IMPERIAL RUSSIAN HISTORY ATLAS

Other books by Martin Gilbert

Winston S. Churchill Volume III 1914–1916
  Companion Volume III (in two parts)
Winston S. Churchill Volume IV 1916–1922
  Companion Volume IV (in three parts)
Winston S. Churchill Volume V 1922–1939
  Companion Volume V (in three parts)
The European Powers 1900–1945
The Roots of Appeasement
Sir Horace Rumbold: Portrait of a Diplomat
Churchill: A Photographic Portrait
Britain and Germany between the Wars
Plough My Own Furrow, the Life of Lord Allen of Hurtwood
Servant of India: Diaries of the Viceroy's Private Secretary
Winston Churchill (Jackdaw)
The Coming of War in 1939 (Jackdaw)
The Second World War
A Century of Conflict: Essays for A. J. P. Taylor
The Appeasers (with Richard Gott)

Other atlases by Martin Gilbert

Recent History Atlas 1860–1960
British History Atlas
American History Atlas
Jewish History Atlas
First World War Atlas
The Arab–Israeli Conflict: Its History in Maps
The Jews of Arab Lands: Their History in Maps
The Jews of Russia: Their History in Maps
Jerusalem: Illustrated History Atlas
Soviet History Atlas

Imperial Russian History Atlas

Martin Gilbert

Fellow of Merton College, Oxford

Cartographic consultant
Arthur Banks

Routledge & Kegan Paul

London and Henley

First published in 1972
by Weidenfeld & Nicolson
as part of the
Russian History Atlas

First published in 1978
by Routledge & Kegan Paul Ltd
39 Store Street,
London WC1E 7DD and
Broadway House,
Newtown Road,
Henley-on-Thames,
Oxon RG9 1EN
Printed in Great Britain by
Morrison and Gibb Ltd, London and Edinburgh
© *Martin Gilbert 1972, 1978*
No part of this book may be reproduced in
any form without permission from the
publisher, except for the quotation of brief
passages in criticism

British Library Cataloguing in Publication Data

Gilbert, Martin

Imperial Russian history atlas.
1. Russia – Historical geography – Maps
I. Title
911'.47   G2111.S1   78–40734

ISBN 0 7100 8962 7
ISBN 0 7100 0084 7   Pbk

Contents

Maps

Preface

It has been my aim in this atlas to present, within the span of ninety maps, a survey of Russian history from the earliest times to the outbreak of the Bolshevik revolution in 1917. In drafting each map I have drawn upon material from a wide range of published sources, encyclopaedias, books, learned articles, atlases and single-sheet maps, each of which I have listed in the bibliography, and to whose authors I am naturally grateful for the information and ideas which they have provided.

On the maps themselves I have tried to include, in addition to the normal information, factual material not usually associated with historical geography, such as the text of Stalin's few surviving personal communications, a postcard which he wrote to his sister from his Siberian exile (printed on Map 54).

I wish to acknowledge the help of many colleagues and friends. In 1962 I began research into Russian history under the supervision of Dr George Katkov, whose insatiable curiosity about elusive historical facts, and whose enthusiasm in tracking them down, have influenced all my subsequent work. I also benefited from the teaching and encouragement of Mr David Footman, Mr Max Hayward, Dr Harry Willetts and the late Mr. Guy Wint. When I was preparing the first sketches for this atlas, the maps I had drawn and the facts I had incorporated on them were scrutinized by three friends— Mr Michael Glenny, Mr Dennis O'Flaherty and Dr Harry Shukman—to each of whom I am most grateful for many detailed suggestions, and for giving up much time to help me. At the outset of my research I received valuable bibliographical advice from Dr J. L. I. Simmons, and suggestions for specific maps from Mr Norman Davies, Dr Ronald Hingley, Mr John B. Kingston and Mr Ewald Uustalu. Jane Cousins helped me with bibliographical and historical research; Mr Arthur Banks transcribed my sketches into clear, printable maps, and Kate Fleming kept a vigilant eye on the cartography. Susie Sacher helped me to compile the index. Sarah Graham, as well as undertaking all the secretarial work, made many important suggestions, factual and cartographic.

I should welcome any suggestions for new maps which could be incorporated in subsequent editions, and any note of errors or obscurities.

Ancient and Early Modern Russia

THE SLAVS BY 800 BC

Probable areas of Slavic settlement by 800 BC

Other tribal groups and peoples by 800 BC

Baltic Sea

BALTS

Dvina

GERMANS

SLAVS

Pripet Marshes

SLAVS

Don

Vistula

Carpathians

SLAVS

Dnieper

Dniester

Volga

Caspian Sea

Danube

Caucasus

Black Sea

GEORGIANS

Byzantium

LAZ

GREEKS

ARMENIANS

Mediterranean

ASSYRIANS

Tigris

MEDES

Euphrates

ARABS

Babylon

Sea

JEWS

Jerusalem

0   300

Miles

The origin of the Slavs is unknown. Possibly they came from the Caucasus. By 800 BC they were probably settled between the Vistula and the Don, in several separate groups

1

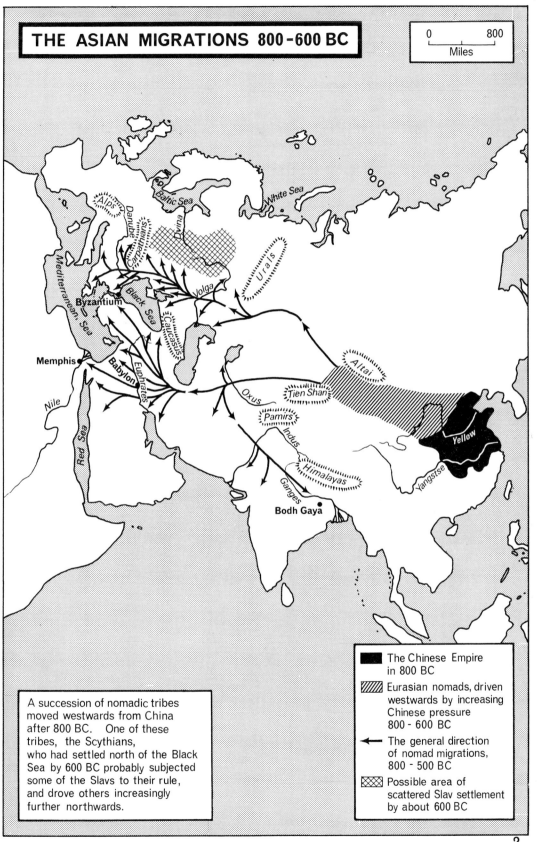

THE ASIAN MIGRATIONS 800-600 BC

0   800
Miles

Baltic Sea
White Sea
Alps
Danube
Dvina
Carpathians
Urals
Volga
Byzantium
Black Sea
Caucasus
Mediterranean Sea
Memphis
Babylon
Euphrates
Altai
Tien Shan
Oxus
Pamirs
Nile
Red Sea
Indus
Himalayas
Yellow
Ganges
Yangstse
Bodh Gaya

The Chinese Empire
in 800 BC

Eurasian nomads, driven
westwards by increasing
Chinese pressure
800 - 600 BC

The general direction
of nomad migrations,
800 - 500 BC

Possible area of
scattered Slav settlement
by about 600 BC

A succession of nomadic tribes
moved westwards from China
after 800 BC.   One of these
tribes, the Scythians,
who had settled north of the Black
Sea by 600 BC probably subjected
some of the Slavs to their rule,
and drove others increasingly
further northwards.

2

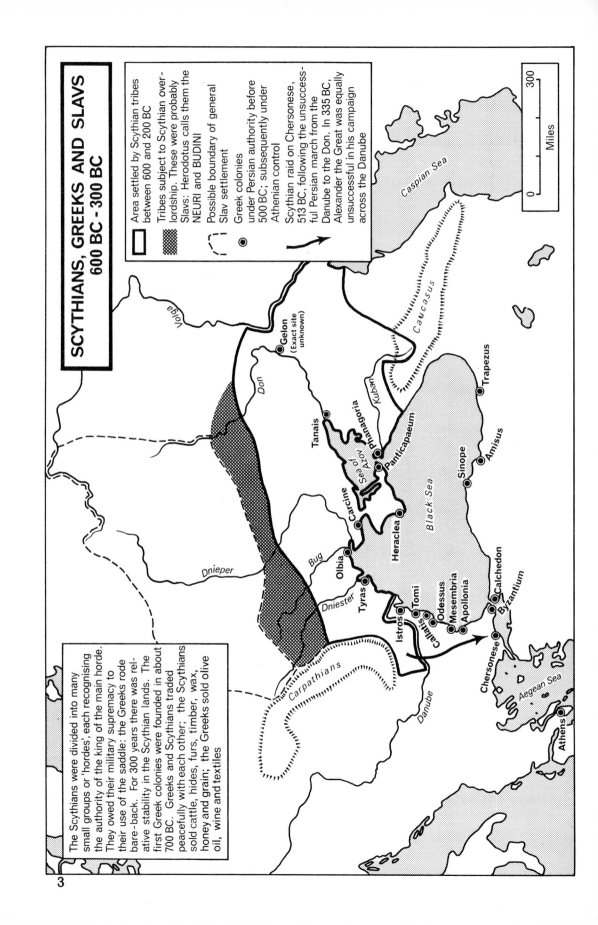

SCYTHIANS, GREEKS AND SLAVS
600 BC - 300 BC

Area settled by Scythian tribes between 600 and 200 BC

Tribes subject to Scythian over-lordship. These were probably Slavs: Herodotus calls them the NEURI and BUDINI

Possible boundary of general Slav settlement

Greek colonies under Persian authority before 500 BC; subsequently under Athenian control

Scythian raid on Chersonese, 513 BC, following the unsuccessful Persian march from the Danube to the Don. In 335 BC, Alexander the Great was equally unsuccessful in his campaign across the Danube

300

0

Miles

The Scythians were divided into many small groups or 'hordes', each recognising the authority of the king of the main horde. They owed their military supremacy to their use of the saddle: the Greeks rode bare-back. For 300 years there was relative stability in the Scythian lands. The first Greek colonies were founded in about 700 BC. Greeks and Scythians traded peacefully with each other; the Scythians sold cattle, hides, furs, timber, wax, honey and grain; the Greeks sold olive oil, wine and textiles

Caspian Sea

Caucasus

Volga

Gelon (Exact site unknown)

Don

Kuban

Tanais

Phanagoria

Panticapaeum

Sea of Azov

Trapezus

Amisus

Sinope

Black Sea

Carcine

Heraclea

Dnieper

Bug

Olbia

Dniester

Tyras

Istros

Tomi

Calatis

Odessus

Mesembria

Apollonia

Byzantium

Calchedon

Chersonese

Carpathians

Danube

Aegean Sea

Athens

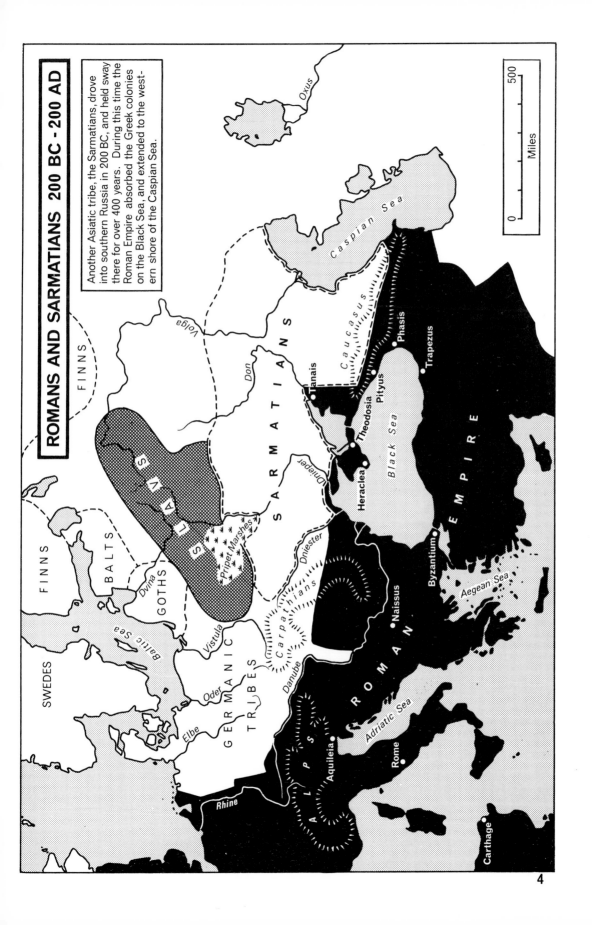

ROMANS AND SARMATIANS 200 BC - 200 AD

Another Asiatic tribe, the Sarmatians, drove into southern Russia in 200 BC, and held sway there for over 400 years. During this time the Roman Empire absorbed the Greek colonies on the Black Sea, and extended to the western shore of the Caspian Sea.

Oxus

Caspian Sea

FINNS

Volga

Don

Caucasus

S A R M A T I A N S

Tanais

Phasis

Trapezus

Theodosia

Pityus

Black Sea

Heraclea

S L A V S

Pripet Marshes

Dnieper

Dniester

FINNS

BALTS

Dvina

GOTHS

Vistula

Oder

Baltic Sea

SWEDES

G E R M A N I C   T R I B E S

Elbe

Carpathians

Danube

Byzantium

Aegean Sea

Naissus

R O M A N

E M P I R E

A L P S

Aquileia

Adriatic Sea

Rome

Rhine

Carthage

500

0

Miles

4

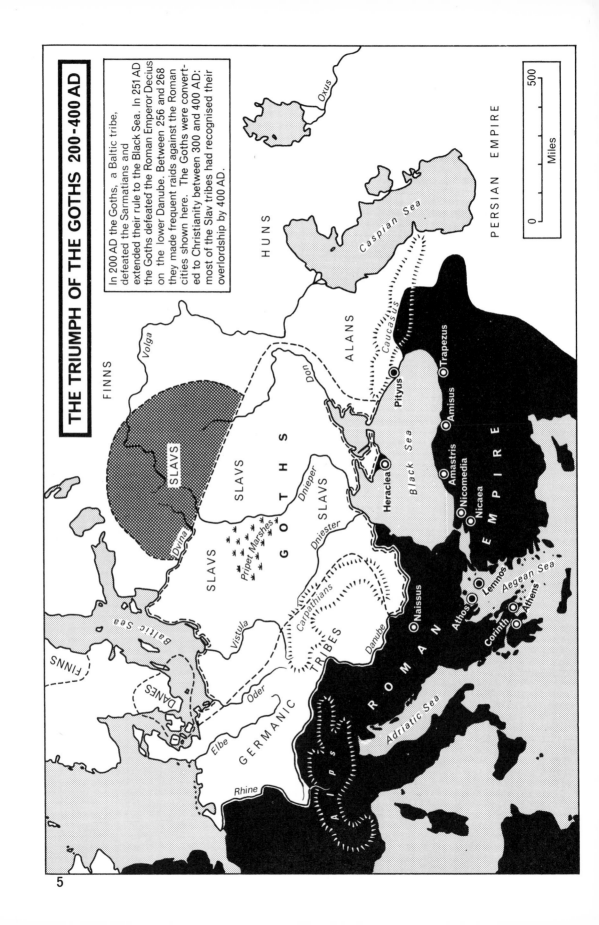

THE TRIUMPH OF THE GOTHS 200-400 AD

In 200 AD the Goths, a Baltic tribe, defeated the Sarmatians and extended their rule to the Black Sea. In 251 AD the Goths defeated the Roman Emperor Decius on the lower Danube. Between 256 and 268 they made frequent raids against the Roman cities shown here. The Goths were converted to Christianity between 300 and 400 AD: most of the Slav tribes had recognised their overlordship by 400 AD.

500

Miles

0

PERSIAN EMPIRE

Oxus

Caspian Sea

HUNS

ALANS

Caucasus

FINNS

Volga

Don

SLAVS

Dvina

SLAVS

SLAVS

GOTHS

Dnieper

Dniester

Pripet Marshes

SLAVS

Trapezus

Pityus

Amisus

Amastris

Nicomedia

Nicaea

Heraclea

Black Sea

Baltic Sea

FINNS

DANES

Vistula

Oder

Elbe

GERMANIC

Carpathians

TRIBES

Danube

Naissus

ROMAN

Athos

Lemnos

Aegean Sea

Corinth

Athens

A l p s

Adriatic Sea

Rhine

EMPIRE

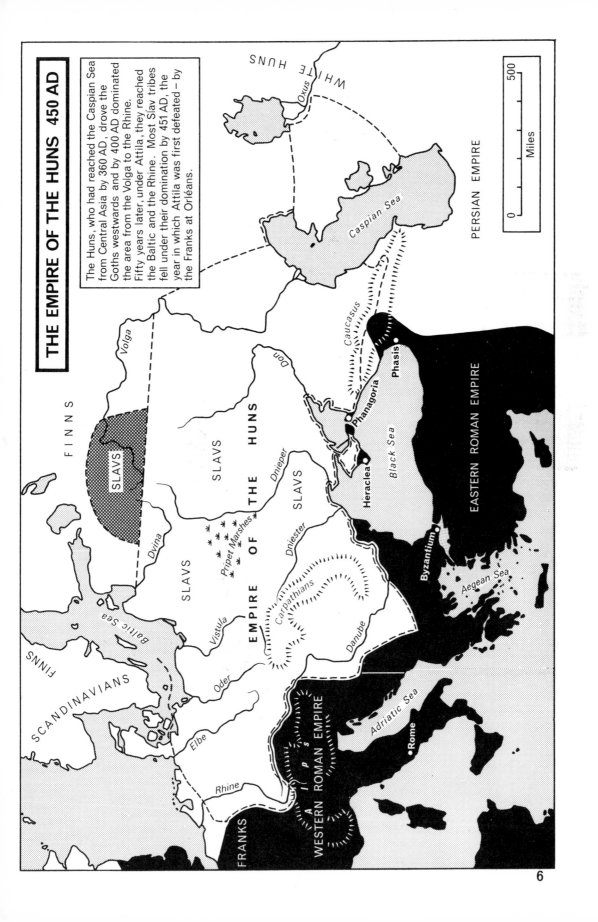

THE EMPIRE OF THE HUNS 450 AD

The Huns, who had reached the Caspian Sea from Central Asia by 360 AD, drove the Goths westwards and by 400 AD dominated the area from the Volga to the Rhine. Fifty years later, under Attila, they reached the Baltic and the Rhine. Most Slav tribes fell under their domination by 451 AD, the year in which Attila was first defeated – by the Franks at Orléans.

WHITE HUNS

PERSIAN EMPIRE

500

0

Miles

FINNS

SLAVS

Volga

Caspian Sea

Oxus

Caucasus

Don

Phasis

Phanagoria

Heraclea

Black Sea

SLAVS

Dnieper

EMPIRE OF THE HUNS

SLAVS

Dniester

Pripet Marshes

EASTERN ROMAN EMPIRE

Byzantium

Aegean Sea

Dvina

SLAVS

Carpathians

Vistula

Danube

FINNS

Baltic Sea

Oder

SCANDINAVIANS

Elbe

Rhine

FRANKS

A l p s

WESTERN ROMAN EMPIRE

Adriatic Sea

Rome

6

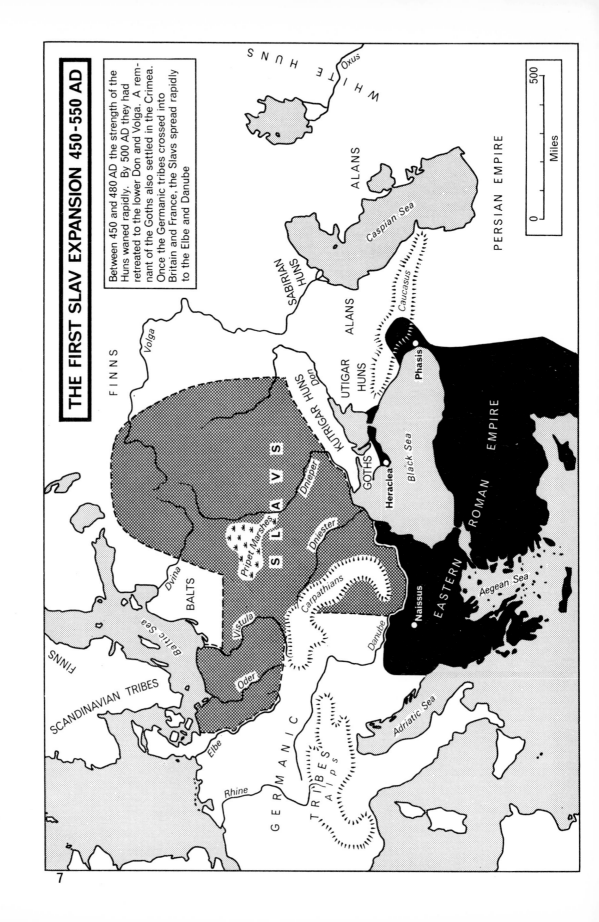

THE FIRST SLAV EXPANSION 450-550 AD

Between 450 and 480 AD the strength of the Huns waned rapidly. By 500 AD they had retreated to the lower Don and Volga. A remnant of the Goths also settled in the Crimea. Once the Germanic tribes crossed into Britain and France, the Slavs spread rapidly to the Elbe and Danube

WHITE HUNS

Oxus

ALANS

PERSIAN EMPIRE

Caspian Sea

0 — 500
Miles

SABIRIAN HUNS

Volga

FINNS

ALANS

Caucasus

Phasis

UTIGAR HUNS

KUTRIGAR HUNS

Don

GOTHS

Black Sea

EASTERN ROMAN EMPIRE

SLAVS

Dnieper

Heraclea

Dniester

Pripet Marshes

BALTS

Carpathians

Aegean Sea

Dvina

Naissus

Vistula

Baltic Sea

Danube

FINNS

Oder

SCANDINAVIAN TRIBES

Adriatic Sea

GERMANIC

TRIBES

Elbe

Alps

Rhine

7

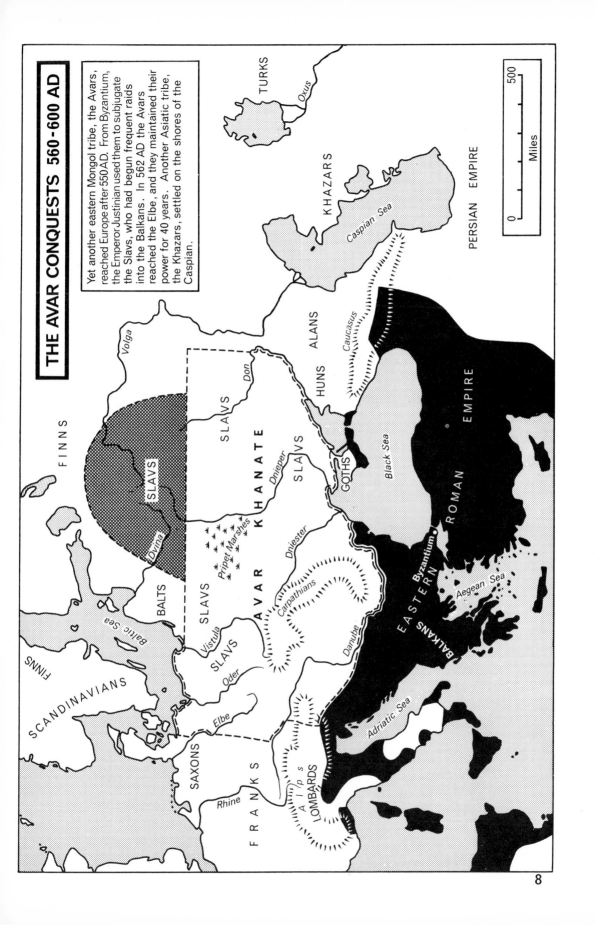

THE AVAR CONQUESTS 560-600 AD

Yet another eastern Mongol tribe, the Avars, reached Europe after 550AD. From Byzantium, the Emperor Justinian used them to subjugate the Slavs, who had begun frequent raids into the Balkans. In 562 AD the Avars reached the Elbe, and they maintained their power for 40 years. Another Asiatic tribe, the Khazars, settled on the shores of the Caspian.

TURKS

Oxus

KHAZARS

Caspian Sea

PERSIAN EMPIRE

500

Miles

0

Volga

FINNS

SLAVS

Don

ALANS

HUNS

Caucasus

SLAVS

SLAVS

Dnieper

ROMAN EMPIRE

GOTHS

Black Sea

K H A N A T E

Pripet Marshes

BALTS

A V A R

Dniester

Carpathians

EASTERN

Byzantium

Aegean Sea

FINNS

Baltic Sea

SLAVS

Vistula

Danube

BALKANS

SCANDINAVIANS

SLAVS

Oder

Adriatic Sea

SAXONS

Elbe

Alps

F R A N K S

Rhine

LOMBARDS

8

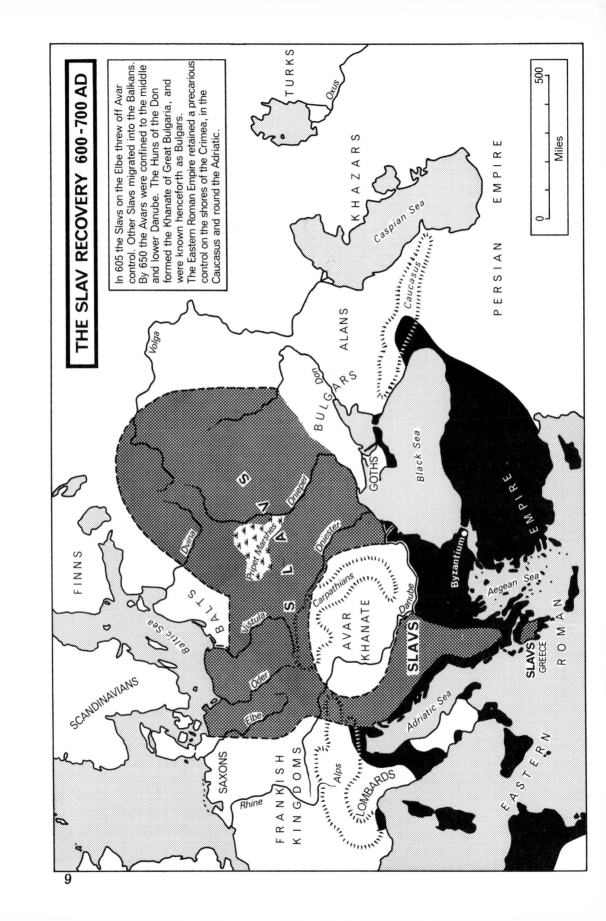

THE SLAV RECOVERY 600-700 AD

In 605 the Slavs on the Elbe threw off Avar control. Other Slavs migrated into the Balkans. By 650 the Avars were confined to the middle and lower Danube. The Huns of the Don formed the Khanate of Great Bulgaria, and were known henceforth as Bulgars. The Eastern Roman Empire retained a precarious control on the shores of the Crimea, in the Caucasus and round the Adriatic.

500

0

Miles

TURKS

Oxus

KHAZARS

Caspian Sea

PERSIAN EMPIRE

Volga

BULGARS

ALANS

Don

Caucasus

GOTHS

Black Sea

FINNS

S L A V S

Dnieper

Dvina

Pripet Marshes

Dniester

BALTS

Baltic Sea

Vistula

Carpathians

AVAR KHANATE

Danube

Byzantium

Aegean Sea

SLAVS

Oder

Elbe

SCANDINAVIANS

SAXONS

FRANKISH KINGDOMS

Rhine

Alps

LOMBARDS

Adriatic Sea

SLAVS

GREECE

ROMAN

EASTERN

EMPIRE

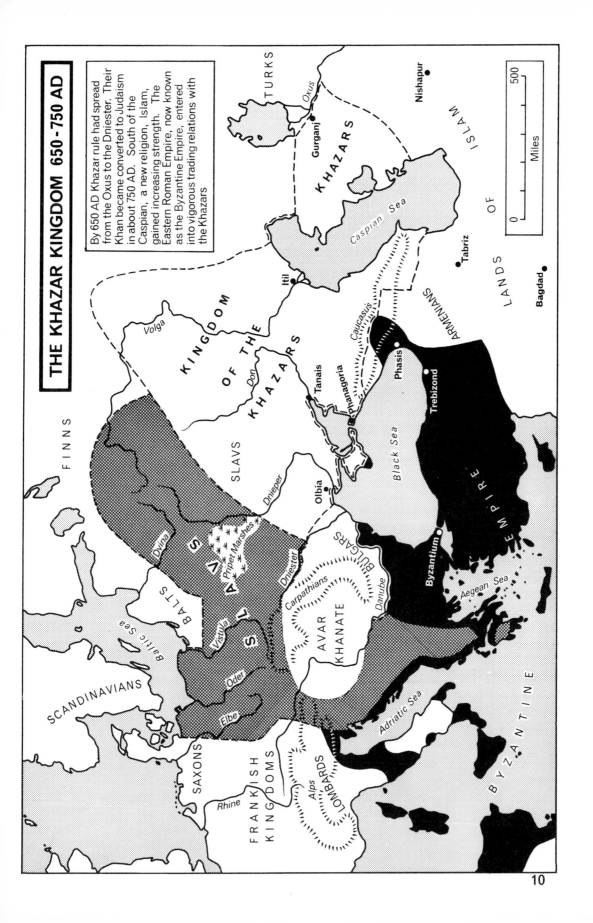

THE KHAZAR KINGDOM 650 - 750 AD

By 650 AD Khazar rule had spread from the Oxus to the Dniester. Their Khan became converted to Judaism in about 750 AD. South of the Caspian, a new religion, Islam, gained increasing strength. The Eastern Roman Empire, now known as the Byzantine Empire, entered into vigorous trading relations with the Khazars

TURKS

KHAZARS

Oxus

Gurganj

Nishapur

Caspian Sea

ISLAM

Itil

KINGDOM

Volga

OF THE

Tabriz

Bagdad

LANDS

OF

KHAZARS

Don

Tanais

Phanagoria

Caucasus

ARMENIANS

SLAVS

Dnieper

Phasis

Trebizond

FINNS

Olbia

Black Sea

Dvina

S

Pripet Marshes

Dniester

BULGARS

Byzantium

BALTS

Vistula

Carpathians

Danube

Aegean Sea

Baltic Sea

S

Oder

AVAR

KHANATE

SCANDINAVIANS

Elbe

Adriatic Sea

SAXONS

FRANKISH
KINGDOMS

Alps

LOMBARDS

B Y Z A N T I N E

Rhine

EMPIRE

500

Miles

0

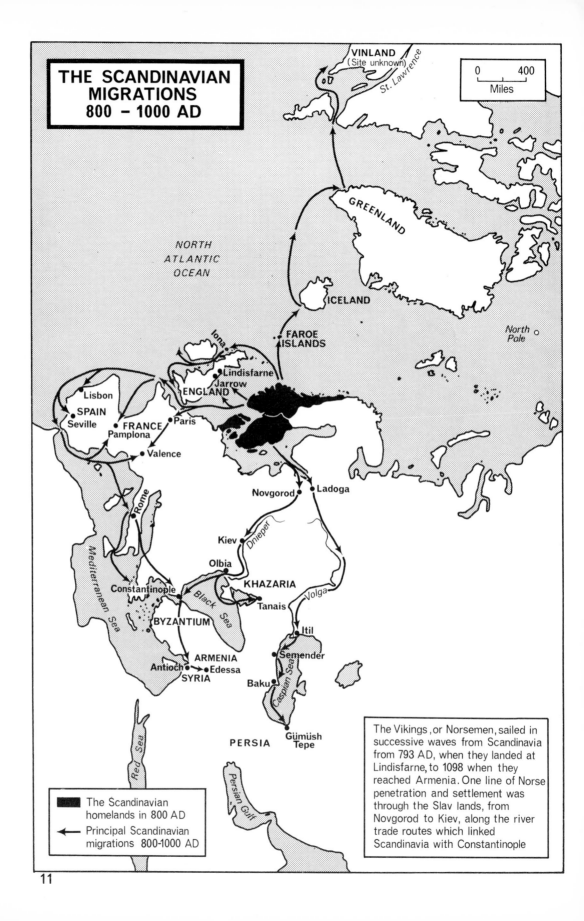

THE SCANDINAVIAN MIGRATIONS 800 – 1000 AD

0   400
Miles

VINLAND
(Site unknown)

St. Lawrence

GREENLAND

NORTH
ATLANTIC
OCEAN

ICELAND

North
Pole

FAROE
ISLANDS

Iona

Lindisfarne
Jarrow
ENGLAND

Lisbon
SPAIN
Seville

FRANCE
Pamplona
Paris

Valence

Rome

Novgorod
Ladoga

Kiev
Dnieper

Mediterranean Sea

Olbia

KHAZARIA

Constantinople

Black Sea

Tanais

Volga

BYZANTIUM

Itil

ARMENIA
Antioch Edessa
SYRIA

Semender

Baku

Caspian Sea

Red Sea

Gümüsh
Tepe

PERSIA

Persian Gulf

The Scandinavian
homelands in 800 AD

Principal Scandinavian
migrations 800-1000 AD

The Vikings, or Norsemen, sailed in
successive waves from Scandinavia
from 793 AD, when they landed at
Lindisfarne, to 1098 when they
reached Armenia. One line of Norse
penetration and settlement was
through the Slav lands, from
Novgorod to Kiev, along the river
trade routes which linked
Scandinavia with Constantinople

THE SLAVS AND THE NORSEMEN BY 880 AD

NORSE

SWEDES

FINNS

DANES

Visby

OBODRICHI

Baltic Sea

BALTS

SLOVIANIANS

Novgorod

CHEREMESIANS

Volga

VIATCHIANS

MORDVINS

POLOCHANE

Smolensk

GERMANS

POLES

Elbe

MAZOVIANS

Pripet Marshes

KRIVICHIANS

SILESIANS

RADIMICHIANS

CZECHS

DEREVLIANS

SEVERIANS

MORAVIANS

Kiev

Don

SLOVAKS

VOLHYNIANS

POLIANIANS

KHAZARS

Danube

SLOVENES

MAGYARS

PECHENEGS

Venice

CROATS

VLACHS

Tmutorokan

Adriatic Sea

SERBS

Black Sea

Caucasus

Preslav

BULGARS

Constantinople

ARMENIANS

Ægean Sea

Athens

GREEKS

The Norse settlers between Novgorod and Kiev quickly dominated the local Slavs, over whom they established political control. Known as "Varangarians", these Norse overlords moulded the Slavs into a coherent federation, "Kievan Rus". Originally Norse speaking, Kievan Rus, or Russia, saw a close mingling of Scandinavian and Slav culture; and the emergence of a strong Kievan, or Russian national consciousness. The first Varangarian ruler, Rurik, led an expedition against Constantinople in 860 AD. His successor Oleg established his capital at Kiev in about 880 AD.

0	300

Miles

12

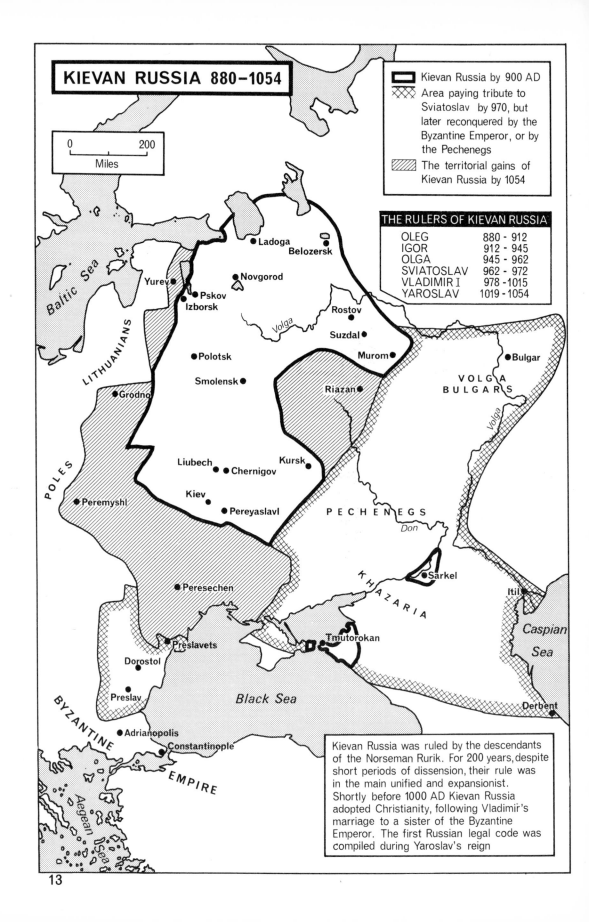

KIEVAN RUSSIA 880–1054

0 — 200 Miles

Kievan Russia by 900 AD

Area paying tribute to Sviatoslav by 970, but later reconquered by the Byzantine Emperor, or by the Pechenegs

The territorial gains of Kievan Russia by 1054

THE RULERS OF KIEVAN RUSSIA

OLEG	880 - 912
IGOR	912 - 945
OLGA	945 - 962
SVIATOSLAV	962 - 972
VLADIMIR I	978 - 1015
YAROSLAV	1019 - 1054

Baltic Sea

Ladoga
Belozersk
Yurev
Novgorod
Pskov
Izborsk
Rostov
Suzdal
Murom
Bulgar
Polotsk
VOLGA BULGARS
Smolensk
Riazan
Volga
LITHUANIANS
Grodno
Liubech
Kursk
Chernigov
Kiev
Pereyaslavl
POLES
PECHENEGS
Don
Peremyshl
Sarkel
KHAZARIA
Itil
Peresechen
Caspian Sea
Preslavets
Tmutorokan
Dorostol
Preslav
Black Sea
Derbent
BYZANTINE
Adrianopolis
Constantinople
EMPIRE
Aegean Sea

Kievan Russia was ruled by the descendants of the Norseman Rurik. For 200 years, despite short periods of dissension, their rule was in the main unified and expansionist. Shortly before 1000 AD Kievan Russia adopted Christianity, following Vladimir's marriage to a sister of the Byzantine Emperor. The first Russian legal code was compiled during Yaroslav's reign

13

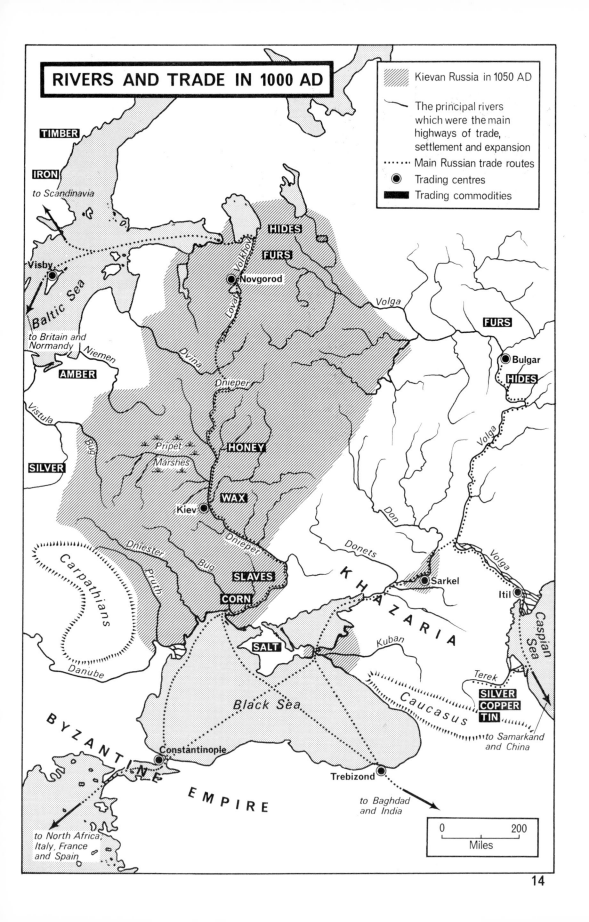

RIVERS AND TRADE IN 1000 AD

Kievan Russia in 1050 AD

The principal rivers which were the main highways of trade, settlement and expansion

Main Russian trade routes

● Trading centres

Trading commodities

TIMBER

IRON

to Scandinavia

Baltic Sea

Visby

to Britain and Normandy

Niemen

AMBER

Vistula

Bug

SILVER

HIDES

FURS

● Novgorod

Volkhov

Lovat

Volga

Dvina

Dnieper

FURS

● Bulgar

HIDES

Volga

Pripet Marshes

HONEY

WAX

Kiev ●

Dnieper

Bug

Prut

Dniester

Carpathians

Danube

SLAVES

CORN

SALT

KHAZARIA

Don

Donets

● Sarkel

Itil ●

Volga

Caspian Sea

Kuban

Terek

Caucasus

SILVER
COPPER
TIN

to Samarkand and China

Black Sea

B Y Z A N T I N E   E M P I R E

Constantinople ●

● Trebizond

to Baghdad and India

to North Africa, Italy, France and Spain

0   200
Miles

14

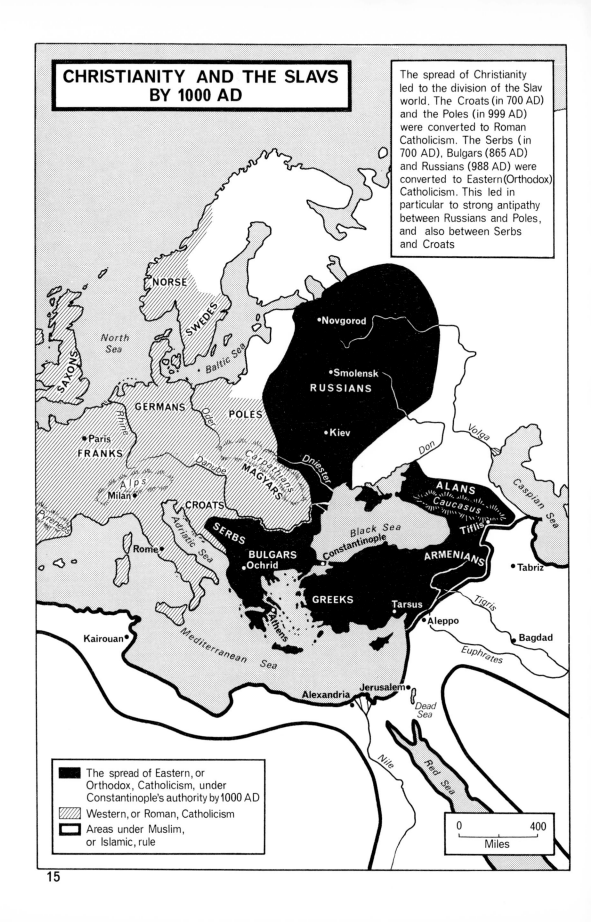

CHRISTIANITY AND THE SLAVS BY 1000 AD

The spread of Christianity led to the division of the Slav world. The Croats (in 700 AD) and the Poles (in 999 AD) were converted to Roman Catholicism. The Serbs (in 700 AD), Bulgars (865 AD) and Russians (988 AD) were converted to Eastern (Orthodox) Catholicism. This led in particular to strong antipathy between Russians and Poles, and also between Serbs and Croats

NORSE

SWEDES

North Sea

Baltic Sea

SAXONS

•Novgorod

•Smolensk

RUSSIANS

GERMANS

Oder

POLES

Rhine

•Paris

FRANKS

Danube

Carpathians

MAGYARS

•Kiev

Dniester

Don

Volga

Alps

Milan•

CROATS

Adriatic Sea

SERBS

BULGARS

•Ochrid

Black Sea

Constantinople

ALANS

Caucasus

Tiflis

Caspian Sea

Rome•

ARMENIANS

•Tabriz

Athens

GREEKS

•Tarsus

Tigris

Kairouan•

Mediterranean Sea

•Aleppo

Euphrates

•Bagdad

Alexandria

Jerusalem•

Dead Sea

Nile

Red Sea

The spread of Eastern, or Orthodox, Catholicism, under Constantinople's authority by 1000 AD

Western, or Roman, Catholicism

Areas under Muslim, or Islamic, rule

0   400
Miles

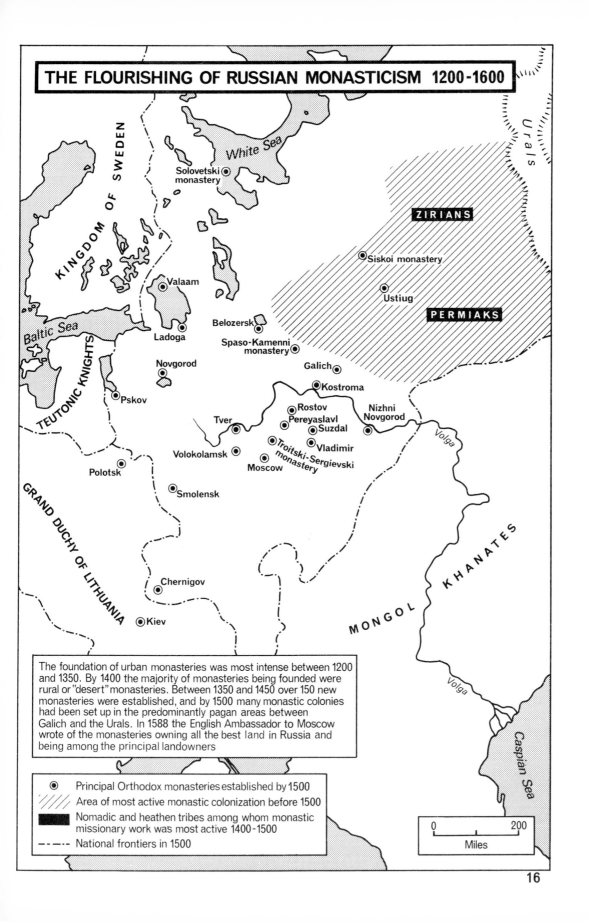

THE FLOURISHING OF RUSSIAN MONASTICISM 1200-1600

KINGDOM OF SWEDEN

White Sea

Solovetski monastery

Urals

ZIRIANS

Siskoi monastery

Ustiug

PERMIAKS

Valaam

Baltic Sea

Belozersk

Spaso-Kamenni monastery

Ladoga

Galich

Novgorod

Kostroma

TEUTONIC KNIGHTS

Pskov

Tver

Rostov
Pereyaslavl
Suzdal

Nizhni Novgorod

Volga

Volokolamsk

Troitski-Sergievski monastery

Vladimir

Polotsk

Moscow

Smolensk

GRAND DUCHY OF LITHUANIA

Chernigov

MONGOL KHANATES

Kiev

Volga

Caspian Sea

The foundation of urban monasteries was most intense between 1200 and 1350. By 1400 the majority of monasteries being founded were rural or "desert" monasteries. Between 1350 and 1450 over 150 new monasteries were established, and by 1500 many monastic colonies had been set up in the predominantly pagan areas between Galich and the Urals. In 1588 the English Ambassador to Moscow wrote of the monasteries owning all the best land in Russia and being among the principal landowners

⊙ Principal Orthodox monasteries established by 1500

///// Area of most active monastic colonization before 1500

▬ Nomadic and heathen tribes among whom monastic missionary work was most active 1400-1500

—·— National frontiers in 1500

0   200
Miles

THE FRAGMENTATION OF KIEVAN RUSSIA 1054–1238

0 — 200
Miles

DEPENDENCIES OF NOVGOROD

FINNS

Ustiug

Ladoga

Belozersk

VLADIMIR–SUZDAL

Reval

REPUBLIC OF NOVGOROD
• Novgorod

Kostroma•
• Yaroslavl
• Rostov

VOLGA BULGARS

Pskov

Torzhok

Izborsk

Tver

• Suzdal

Riga

Dvina

Moscow

Vladimir

Polotsk

SMOLENSK

Murom

LITHUANIA

Vitebsk

Viazma
• Smolensk

Riazan

MUROM–RIAZAN

Kovno •

POLOTSK
• Minsk

CHERNIGOV

Vistula

TUROV
• Pinsk

NOVGOROD–SEVERSK

POLAND

• Bialystok

Turov

Chernigov

VOLHYNIA

KIEV
Kiev

PEREYASLAVL
• Pereyaslavl

Cracow

• Zhitomir

GALICIA
•Galich

Don

Carpathians

Dniester

CUMANS or POLOVTSI

HUNGARY

Black Sea

Constantinople

On the death of Yaroslav in 1054, Kievan Russia was divided among his sons. Their constant feuds led to the fragmentation of the once powerful kingdom. United briefly from 1113 to 1125 by Vladimir Monomakh, the Russian lands were again divided and in conflict during the hundred years before the Mongol invasion of 1238. In 1199 Galicia and Volhynia were united, and in 1254 recognised by the Pope as an independent kingdom. In 1307 Polotsk came under Lithuanian suzerainty

☐ The twelve Principalities of Russia in 1100

17

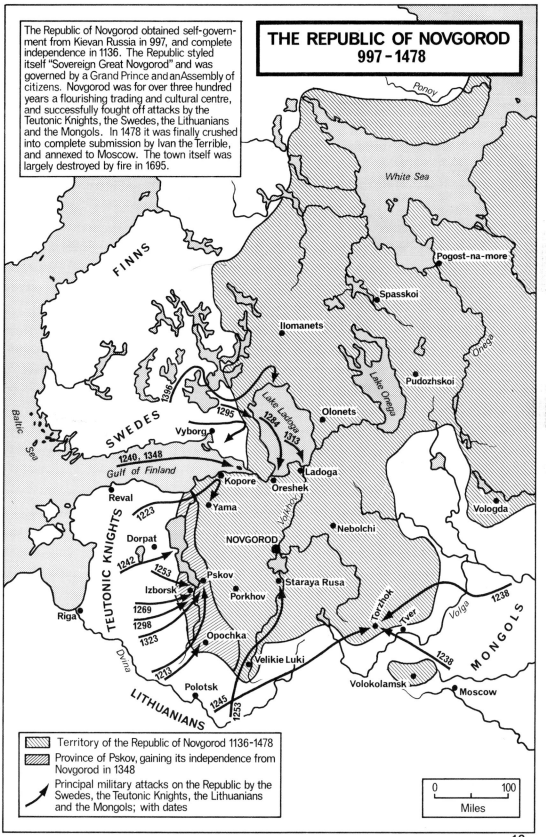

The Republic of Novgorod obtained self-government from Kievan Russia in 997, and complete
independence in 1136. The Republic styled
itself "Sovereign Great Novgorod" and was
governed by a Grand Prince and an Assembly of
citizens. Novgorod was for over three hundred
years a flourishing trading and cultural centre,
and successfully fought off attacks by the
Teutonic Knights, the Swedes, the Lithuanians
and the Mongols. In 1478 it was finally crushed
into complete submission by Ivan the Terrible,
and annexed to Moscow. The town itself was
largely destroyed by fire in 1695.

THE REPUBLIC OF NOVGOROD
997 – 1478

Ponoy

White Sea

Pogost-na-more

Spasskoi

FINNS

Ilomanets

Lake Onega

Pudozhskoi

Onega

1396

1295

Lake Ladoga

1284

Olonets

SWEDES

Vyborg

1313

Baltic Sea

1240, 1348

Gulf of Finland

Ladoga

Vologda

Kopore

Oreshek

Reval

Yama

Volkhov

1223

Nebolchi

NOVGOROD

Dorpat

1242

Pskov

Staraya Rusa

Riga

1253

Izborsk

Porkhov

TEUTONIC KNIGHTS

1269

Torzhok

1238

1298

Volga

Tver

1323

Opochka

MONGOLS

Dvina

1213

Velikie Luki

1238

Volokolamsk

LITHUANIANS

1245

Polotsk

1253

Moscow

Territory of the Republic of Novgorod 1136-1478

Province of Pskov, gaining its independence from
Novgorod in 1348

Principal military attacks on the Republic by the
Swedes, the Teutonic Knights, the Lithuanians
and the Mongols; with dates

| 0 | 100 |

Miles

18

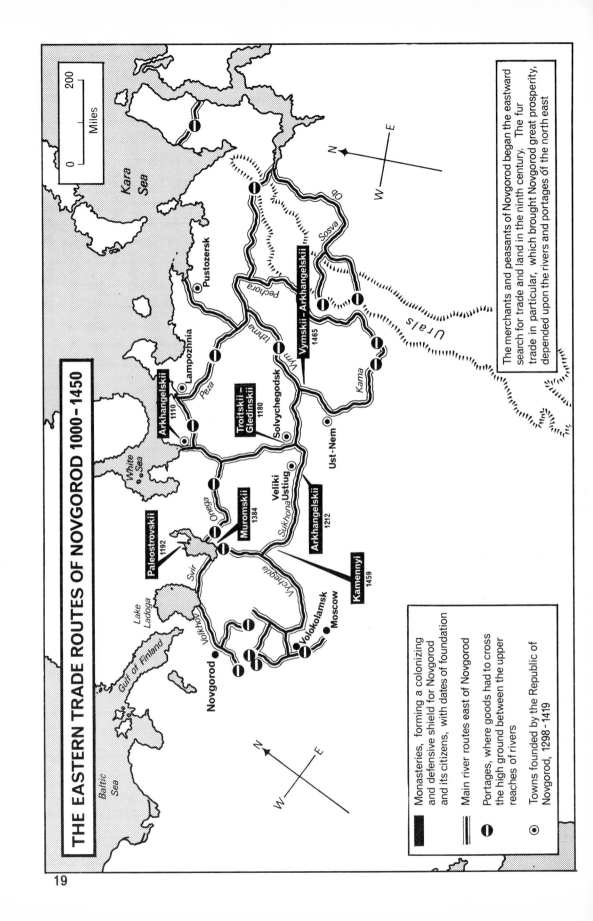

THE EASTERN TRADE ROUTES OF NOVGOROD 1000-1450

The merchants and peasants of Novgorod began the eastward search for trade and land in the ninth century. The fur trade in particular, which brought Novgorod great prosperity, depended upon the rivers and portages of the north east

Monasteries, forming a colonizing and defensive shield for Novgorod and its citizens, with dates of foundation

Main river routes east of Novgorod

Portages, where goods had to cross the high ground between the upper reaches of rivers

Towns founded by the Republic of Novgorod, 1298-1419

Kara Sea

Pustozersk

Lampozhnia

Arkhangelskii 1110

Troitskii – Gledinskii 1180

Vymskii – Arkhangelskii 1465

Solvychegodsk

Ust-Nem

White Sea

Veliki Ustiug

Arkhangelskii 1212

Paleostrovskii 1192

Muromskii 1384

Kamennyi 1459

Lake Ladoga

Volokolamsk

Moscow

Novgorod

Gulf of Finland

Baltic Sea

Ob

Sosva

Pechora

Izhma

Vym

Kama

Peza

Svir

Onega

Sukhona

Vychegda

Volkhov

Urals

0

200

Miles

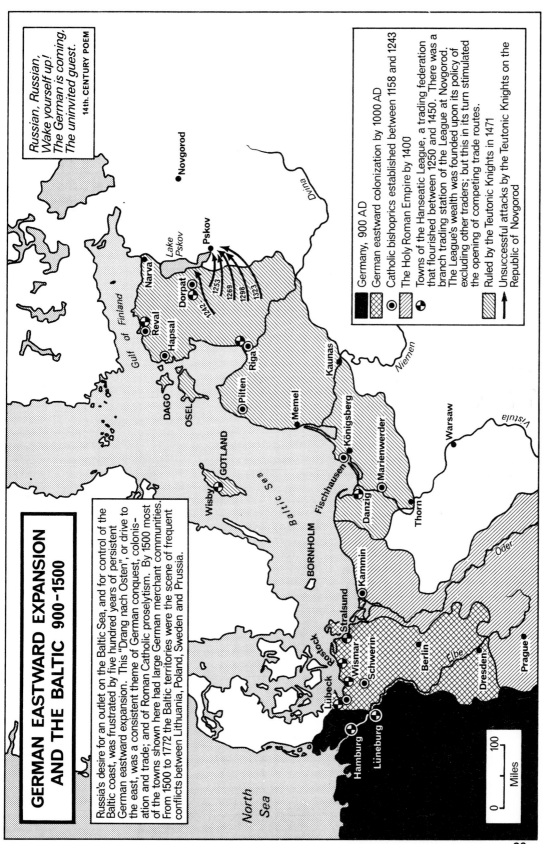

GERMAN EASTWARD EXPANSION AND THE BALTIC 900–1500

Russia's desire for an outlet on the Baltic Sea, and for control of the Baltic coast, was frustrated by five hundred years of persistent German eastward expansion. This "Drang nach Osten", or drive to the east, was a consistent theme of German conquest, colonisation and trade; and of Roman Catholic proselytism. By 1500 most of the towns shown here had large German merchant communities. From 1500 to 1772 the Baltic territories were the scene of frequent conflicts between Lithuania, Poland, Sweden and Prussia.

Russian, Russian,
Wake yourself up!
The German is coming,
The uninvited guest.
14th. CENTURY POEM

Germany, 900 AD

German eastward colonization by 1000 AD

Catholic bishoprics established between 1158 and 1243

The Holy Roman Empire by 1400

Towns of the Hanseatic League, a trading federation that flourished between 1250 and 1450. There was a branch trading station of the League at Novgorod. The League's wealth was founded upon its policy of excluding other traders; but this in its turn stimulated the opening of competing trade routes.

Ruled by the Teutonic Knights in 1471

Unsuccessful attacks by the Teutonic Knights on the Republic of Novgorod

North Sea

Hamburg
Lüneburg
Lübeck
Rostock
Wismar
Schwerin
Straslund
Berlin
Dresden
Prague
Elbe
Oder
Kammin
BORNHOLM
Danzig
Thorn
Warsaw
Vistula
Marienwerder
Königsberg
Fischhausen
GOTLAND
Wisby
Baltic Sea
Memel
Kaunas
Niemen
Pilten
OSEL
DAGO
Riga
Hapsal
Reval
Narva
Dorpat
Lake Pskov
Pskov
1242
1253
1269
1298
1323
Divina
Novgorod
Gulf of Finland

0   100
Miles

20

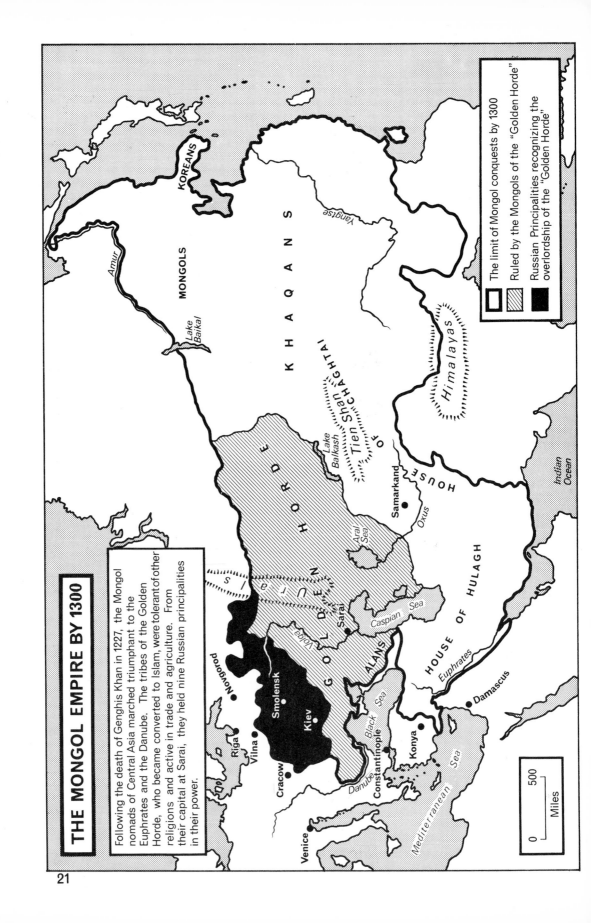

THE MONGOL EMPIRE BY 1300

Following the death of Genghis Khan in 1227, the Mongol nomads of Central Asia marched triumphant to the Euphrates and the Danube. The tribes of the Golden Horde, who became converted to Islam, were tolerant of other religions and active in trade and agriculture. From their capital at Sarai, they held nine Russian principalities in their power.

The limit of Mongol conquests by 1300

Ruled by the Mongols of the "Golden Horde"

Russian Principalities recognizing the overlordship of the "Golden Horde"

KOREANS

MONGOLS

Amur

Lake Baikal

Yangtse

K H A Q A N S

Himalayas

Tien Shan

CHAGHTAI

O F

H O U S E

Lake Balkash

Samarkand

Oxus

Indian Ocean

S I B E R I A

G O L D E N   H O R D E

Aral Sea

Caspian Sea

HOUSE OF HULAGH

Euphrates

Volga

Sarai

ALANS

Damascus

Novgorod

Smolensk

Kiev

Riga

Vilna

Black Sea

Cracow

Danube

Constantinople

Konya

Venice

Mediterranean Sea

0   500

Miles

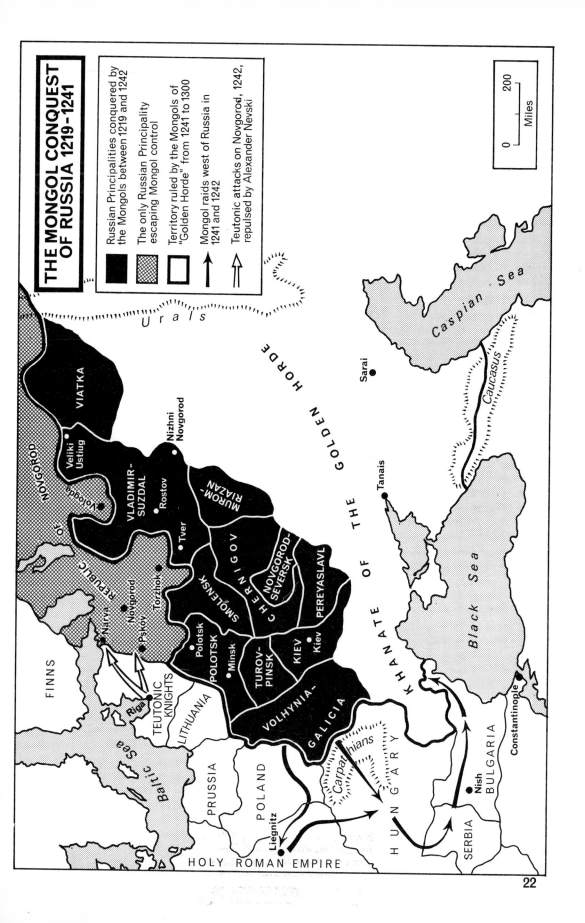

THE MONGOL CONQUEST OF RUSSIA 1219-1241

Russian Principalities conquered by the Mongols between 1219 and 1242

The only Russian Principality escaping Mongol control

Territory ruled by the Mongols of "Golden Horde" from 1241 to 1300

Mongol raids west of Russia in 1241 and 1242

Teutonic attacks on Novgorod, 1242, repulsed by Alexander Nevski

200

0

Miles

Caspian Sea

U r a l s

VIATKA

Sarai

Veliki Ustiug

Nizhni Novgorod

VLADIMIR-SUZDAL

Rostov

NOVGOROD

Vologda

MUROM-RIAZAN

Tver

GOLDEN

Tanais

THE

Caucasus

KHANATE

OF

CHERNIGOV

NOVGOROD-SEVERSK

PEREYASLAVL

REPUBLIC

SMOLENSK

Novgorod

Torzhok

Pskov

Narva

POLOTSK

Polotsk

Minsk

TUROV-PINSK

KIEV

Kiev

Black Sea

FINNS

TEUTONIC KNIGHTS

Riga

LITHUANIA

VOLHYNIA-GALICIA

Constantinople

Baltic Sea

PRUSSIA

POLAND

Carpathians

H U N G A R Y

BULGARIA

Nish

SERBIA

Liegnitz

HOLY ROMAN EMPIRE

THE LITHUANIAN CONQUESTS 1240 - 1462

Baltic Sea

ROSTOV

NOVGOROD

TVER

PSKOV

MOSCOW

Riga

TEUTONIC KNIGHTS

Polotsk

Viazma

Vitebsk

Smolensk

Kovno

Vilna

TEUTONIC KNIGHTS

Minsk

Briansk

RIAZAN

Grodno

Slonim

Warsaw

Brest-Litovsk

Turov

Pinsk

Chernigov

KINGDOM

Vladimir

OF

Kiev

POLAND

Zhitomir

Poltava

Lvov

CRIMEAN KHANATE
Mongols

CRIMEAN KHANATE
Mongols

0   150

Miles

Haji-bey

Black Sea

Sea of Azov

Grand Principality of Lithuania, 1240

Lithuanian conquests by 1340, including
the Russian Principalities of Polotsk
and Pinsk-Turov

Ruled by Lithuania in 1462

Russian Principalities unconquered
by Lithuania

Shattered by Mongol invasions, and
divided among themselves, the Russian
Principalities fell easy victims to Lithuanian
expansion after 1240.
In 1386, Lithuania and the Kingdom of
Poland united under a single king. The
Catholicism of this powerful kingdom was
an extra cause of conflict with Russia.

THE EASTWARD SPREAD OF CATHOLICISM BY 1462

Simultaneously with the Mongol invasions from the east, Russia was subjected to the continual westward movement of Roman Catholicism. Under Swedish and Lithuanian pressure, Russian Orthodoxy was pushed back almost to Moscow. Roman Catholicism also made advances against the Orthodox Bulgars in the Balkans, and against the Muslim lands in the eastern Mediterranean.

LAPLAND
1300

NORWAY

SWEDEN

DENMARK

Baltic Sea

Vyborg
1293

Reval
1219

Pskov

Mitava
1271

Danzig
1200

PRUSSIA

Vilna
1386

Warsaw

POLAND

Prague

BOHEMIA

GALICIA

Lvov
1340

Vienna

HUNGARY

CROATIA

TRANSYLVANIA

THE

HOLY

ROMAN

EMPIRE

RUSSIA

Novgorod

Tver

Moscow

Kaluga

Smolensk
1450

LITHUANIA

Kiev
1385

UKRAINE

Tana
1261

Kaffa
1261

Black Sea

BALKANS

Rome

Constantinople
1261

Amastris
1310

Samsun
1310

Athens
1305

Aegean Sea

Edessa
1098

Antioch
1098

■ The Roman Catholic world in 1000 AD

▨ Conquered between 1000 and 1462 AD by Roman Catholic rulers, and forming part of Catholic kingdoms

0   300
Miles

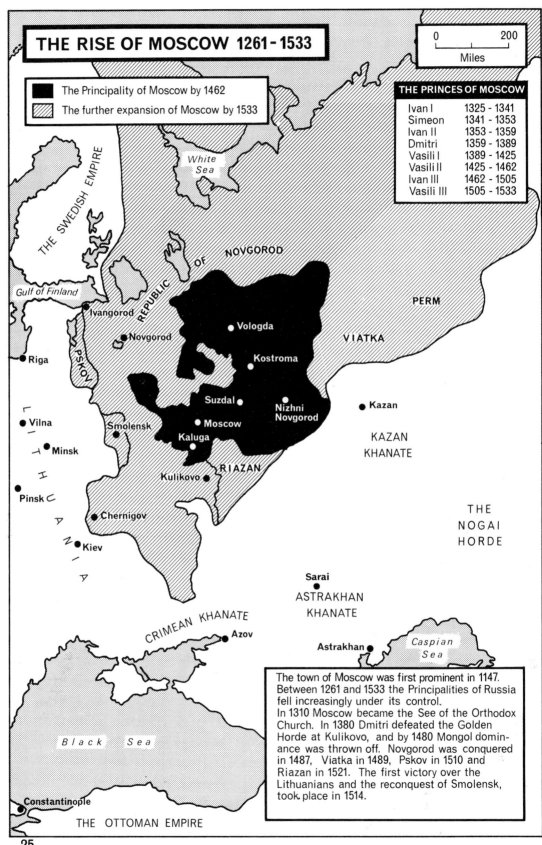

THE RISE OF MOSCOW 1261-1533

0	200

Miles

■ The Principality of Moscow by 1462

▨ The further expansion of Moscow by 1533

THE PRINCES OF MOSCOW

Ivan I	1325 - 1341
Simeon	1341 - 1353
Ivan II	1353 - 1359
Dmitri	1359 - 1389
Vasili I	1389 - 1425
Vasili II	1425 - 1462
Ivan III	1462 - 1505
Vasili III	1505 - 1533

THE SWEDISH EMPIRE

White Sea

Gulf of Finland

REPUBLIC OF NOVGOROD

PERM

● Ivangorod

● Novgorod

PSKOV

● Vologda

VIATKA

● Riga

● Kostroma

● Vilna

● Suzdal

● Nizhni Novgorod

● Kazan

● Smolensk

● Moscow

KAZAN KHANATE

● Minsk

● Kaluga

● Pinsk

RIAZAN

L I T H U A N I A

● Kulikovo

THE NOGAI HORDE

● Chernigov

● Kiev

● Sarai

ASTRAKHAN KHANATE

CRIMEAN KHANATE

● Azov

Astrakhan ●

Caspian Sea

Black   Sea

The town of Moscow was first prominent in 1147. Between 1261 and 1533 the Principalities of Russia fell increasingly under its control.
In 1310 Moscow became the See of the Orthodox Church. In 1380 Dmitri defeated the Golden Horde at Kulikovo, and by 1480 Mongol domin- ance was thrown off. Novgorod was conquered in 1487, Viatka in 1489, Pskov in 1510 and Riazan in 1521. The first victory over the Lithuanians and the reconquest of Smolensk, took place in 1514.

● Constantinople

THE OTTOMAN EMPIRE

25

THE EXPANSION OF RUSSIA 1533-1598

☐ Russia in 1533

← Unsuccessful military expedition against the Mongols of the Crimea 1556-1559

▨ Russian conquests by 1598

◉ Cities founded 1584-1594, with dates

Arctic Sea

SWEDISH EMPIRE

◉ Archangel 1584

Baltic Sea

◉ Kexholm

INGRIA

● Pskov

Dvina

◉ Surgut 1594

◉ Obski Gorodok 1585

SIBERIA

Urals

Ob

◉ Tobolsk 1587

Tiumen ◉ 1586

● Polotsk

LITHUANIA

● Smolensk

● Moscow

Volga

● Kazan

● Chernigov

● Kiev

◉ Voronezh 1586

◉ Samara 1586

Volga

◉ Saratov 1590

THE NOGAI HORDE

CRIMEAN KHANATE

◉ Tsaritsyn 1589

● Bakhchisaray

Black Sea

Astrakhan ●

Terek

Caucasus

Caspian Sea

OTTOMAN EMPIRE

Ivan IV became Grand Duke of Moscow in 1533. In 1547 he was crowned "Tsar of All the Russias". He conquered the Mongol Khanate of Kazan in 1552, the Khanate of Astrakhan in 1556, and the Mongols east of the Urals in 1584. In 1583 the Swedes conquered Ingria and Russia lost all access to the Baltic Sea; but this was regained under Tsar Fedor, 1584-1598.

0 ─── 400

Miles

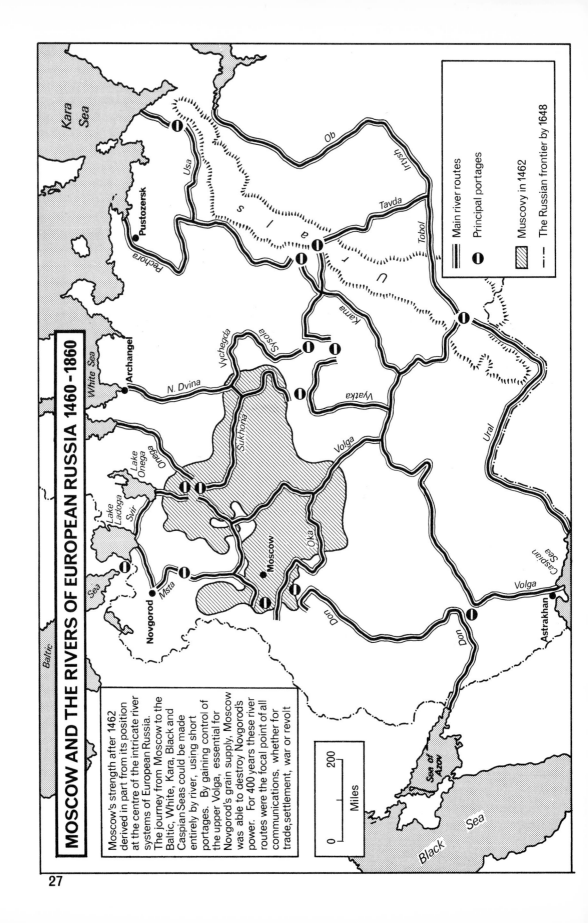

MOSCOW AND THE RIVERS OF EUROPEAN RUSSIA 1460 – 1860

Moscow's strength after 1462 derived in part from its position at the centre of the intricate river systems of European Russia. The journey from Moscow to the Baltic, White, Kara, Black and Caspian Seas could be made entirely by river, using short portages. By gaining control of the upper Volga, essential for Novgorod's grain supply, Moscow was able to destroy Novgorod's power. For 400 years these river routes were the focal point of all communications, whether for trade, settlement, war or revolt

Legend:
- Main river routes
- Principal portages
- Muscovy in 1462
- The Russian frontier by 1648

Miles
0   200

Kara Sea
Baltic Sea
White Sea
Black Sea
Sea of Azov
Caspian Sea
Lake Ladoga
Lake Onega
Siberia
Urals

Pustozersk
Archangel
Novgorod
Moscow
Astrakhan

Ob
Irtysh
Tavda
Tobol
Usa
Pechora
Kama
Vychegda
Sysola
N. Dvina
Vyatka
Ural
Sukhona
Onega
Svir
Msta
Volga
Oka
Don
Volga

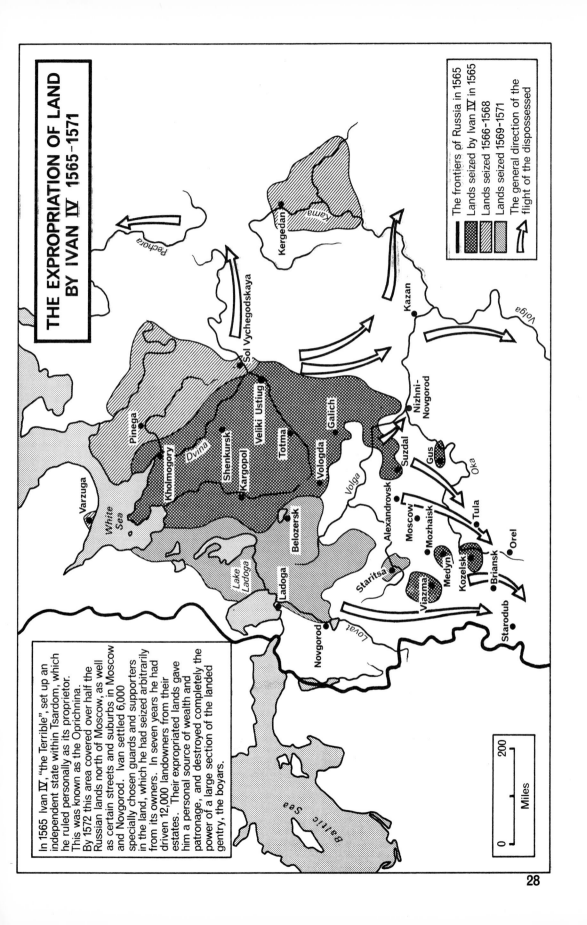

THE EXPROPRIATION OF LAND BY IVAN IV 1565-1571

In 1565 Ivan IV, "the Terrible", set up an independent state within Tsardom, which he ruled personally as its proprietor. This was known as the Oprichnina.
By 1572 this area covered over half the Russian lands north of Moscow, as well as certain streets and suburbs in Moscow and Novgorod. Ivan settled 6,000 specially chosen guards and supporters in the land, which he had seized arbitrarily from its owners. In seven years he had driven 12,000 landowners from their estates. Their expropriated lands gave him a personal source of wealth and patronage, and destroyed completely the power of a large section of the landed gentry, the boyars.

The frontiers of Russia in 1565
Lands seized by Ivan IV in 1565
Lands seized 1566–1568
Lands seized 1569–1571
The general direction of the flight of the dispossessed

0   200
Miles

Varzuga
White Sea
Pinega
Kholmogory
Dvina
Shenkursk
Kargopol
Veliki Ustiug
Totma
Vologda
Galich
Belozersk
Sol Vychegodskaya
Kergedan
Kama
Pechora
Lake Ladoga
Ladoga
Novgorod
Lovat
Starodub
Briansk
Orel
Kozelsk
Medyn
Viazma
Staritsa
Mozhaisk
Moscow
Alexandrovsk
Suzdal
Gus
Tula
Oka
Nizhni-Novgorod
Kazan
Volga
Volga
Baltic Sea

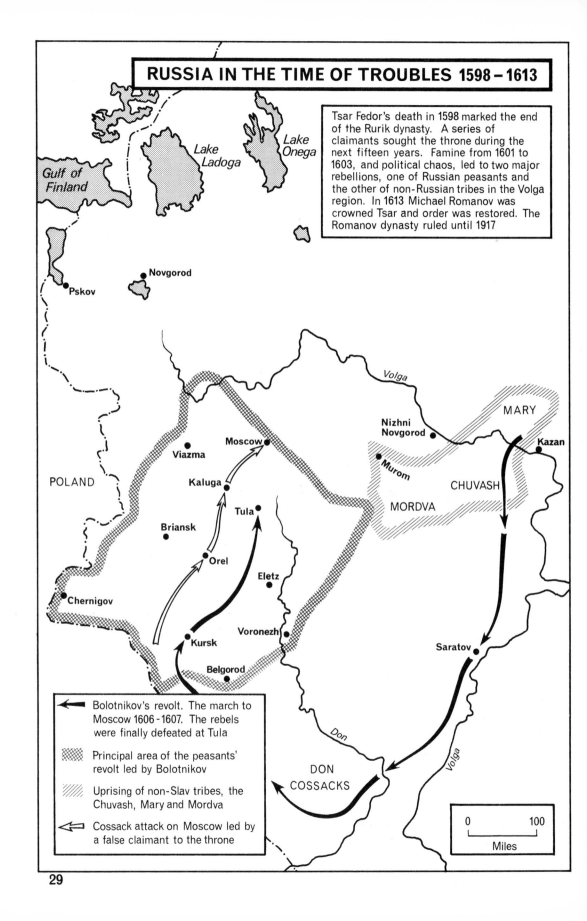

RUSSIA IN THE TIME OF TROUBLES 1598 – 1613

Tsar Fedor's death in 1598 marked the end of the Rurik dynasty. A series of claimants sought the throne during the next fifteen years. Famine from 1601 to 1603, and political chaos, led to two major rebellions, one of Russian peasants and the other of non-Russian tribes in the Volga region. In 1613 Michael Romanov was crowned Tsar and order was restored. The Romanov dynasty ruled until 1917

Gulf of Finland

Lake Ladoga

Lake Onega

Novgorod

Pskov

Volga

Nizhni Novgorod

MARY

Kazan

Moscow

Viazma

Murom

CHUVASH

Kaluga

MORDVA

POLAND

Tula

Briansk

Orel

Eletz

Chernigov

Voronezh

Saratov

Kursk

Belgorod

Don

Volga

DON COSSACKS

← Bolotnikov's revolt. The march to Moscow 1606 - 1607. The rebels were finally defeated at Tula

⟨hatched⟩ Principal area of the peasants' revolt led by Bolotnikov

⟨hatched⟩ Uprising of non-Slav tribes, the Chuvash, Mary and Mordva

⟸ Cossack attack on Moscow led by a false claimant to the throne

0   100
Miles

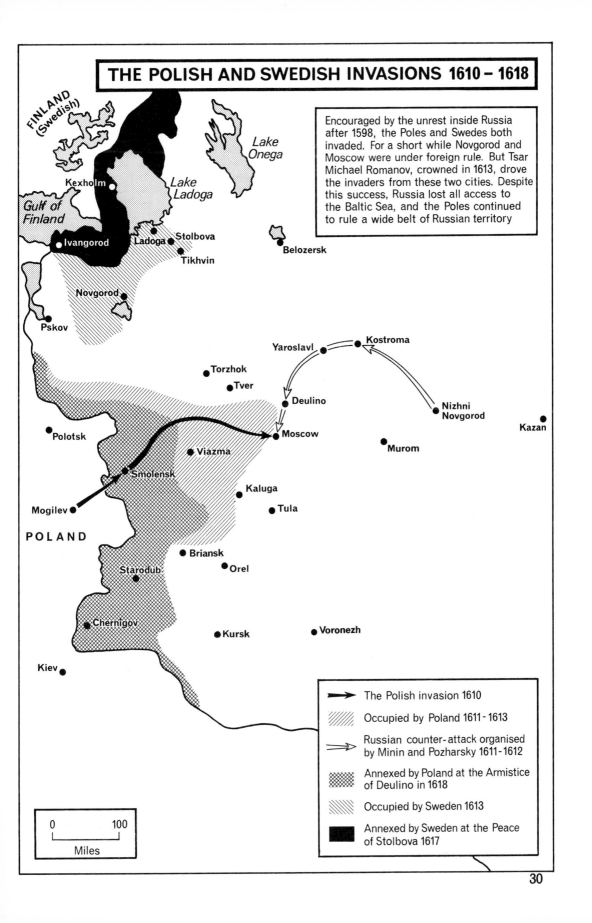

THE POLISH AND SWEDISH INVASIONS 1610 – 1618

FINLAND
(Swedish)

Lake Onega

Kexholm

Lake Ladoga

Gulf of Finland

Encouraged by the unrest inside Russia after 1598, the Poles and Swedes both invaded. For a short while Novgorod and Moscow were under foreign rule. But Tsar Michael Romanov, crowned in 1613, drove the invaders from these two cities. Despite this success, Russia lost all access to the Baltic Sea, and the Poles continued to rule a wide belt of Russian territory

Ivangorod

Ladoga
Stolbova

Tikhvin

Belozersk

Novgorod

Pskov

Yaroslavl
Kostroma

Torzhok

Tver

Deulino

Nizhni Novgorod

Moscow

Kazan

Polotsk

Viazma

Murom

Smolensk

Kaluga

Mogilev

Tula

POLAND

Briansk

Orel

Starodub

Chernigov

Kursk

Voronezh

Kiev

	The Polish invasion 1610
	Occupied by Poland 1611-1613
	Russian counter-attack organised by Minin and Pozharsky 1611-1612
	Annexed by Poland at the Armistice of Deulino in 1618
	Occupied by Sweden 1613
	Annexed by Sweden at the Peace of Stolbova 1617

0   100
Miles

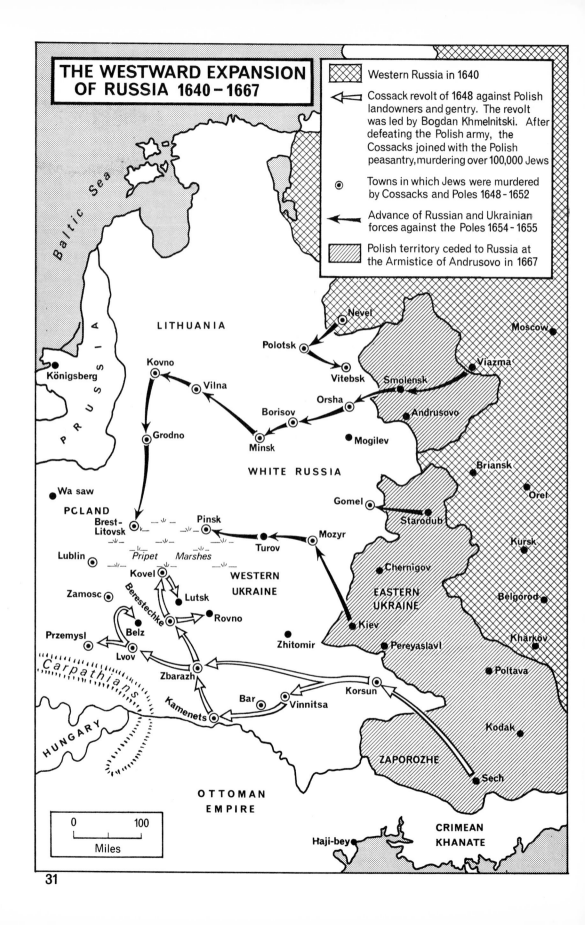

THE WESTWARD EXPANSION OF RUSSIA 1640-1667

Western Russia in 1640

Cossack revolt of 1648 against Polish landowners and gentry. The revolt was led by Bogdan Khmelnitski. After defeating the Polish army, the Cossacks joined with the Polish peasantry, murdering over 100,000 Jews

Towns in which Jews were murdered by Cossacks and Poles 1648-1652

Advance of Russian and Ukrainian forces against the Poles 1654-1655

Polish territory ceded to Russia at the Armistice of Andrusovo in 1667

Baltic Sea

PRUSSIA

LITHUANIA

Nevel

Moscow

Königsberg

Polotsk

Vitebsk

Smolensk

Viazma

Kovno

Vilna

Orsha

Andrusovo

Borisov

Grodno

Minsk

Mogilev

Brainsk

WHITE RUSSIA

Orel

Wa saw

Gomel

Starodub

POLAND

Brest-Litovsk

Pinsk

Mozyr

Kursk

Turov

Lublin

Pripet Marshes

Chernigov

EASTERN UKRAINE

Belgorod

Kovel

WESTERN UKRAINE

Zamosc

Berestechke

Lutsk

Rovno

Przemysl

Belz

Zhitomir

Kiev

Kharkov

Lvov

Zbarazh

Pereyaslavl

Poltava

Carpathians

Kamenets

Bar

Vinnitsa

Korsun

Kodak

HUNGARY

ZAPOROZHE

Sech

OTTOMAN EMPIRE

0   100

Miles

CRIMEAN KHANATE

Haji-bey

SOCIAL UNREST 1648 and 1670

In 1648 uprisings took place in many of the principal Russian towns. As a result, a new code of laws was drawn up, protecting the rights of traders and town-dwellers. In 1670 a Don Cossack, Stenka Razin, led a widespread revolt of Cossacks, peasants, small traders, minor officials and the dispossessed of the Volga, Don and Donets river valleys. The revolt was crushed in 1671 and Razin broken on the wheel in Moscow.

◉ Kargopol

◉ Solvychegodsk
◉ Veliki Ustiug   ◉ Cherdin
◉ Olonets
                                   ◉ Solikamsk
Totma ◉

◉ Gdov
◉ Ps" Pskov   ◉ Novgorod
◉ Ostrov
                    ◉ Romanov

                      Volga
            Vladimir ◉
    Ruza ◉   ◉
          Moscow   Yadrin ●

                          Simbirsk ●
              Koslov
                    Penza ●
              ◉ Tambov

                              Samara
    Kursk ◉   *Donets*
    Voronezh ◉   Saratov ●
        Don

                    Tsaritsyn ●
              D O N
              CO   SSACKS   Gurev ●

        Sea of
        Azov   Astrakhan ○

                                   Caspian Sea

    Black   Sea   Terski
                         Gorodok ●

◉   Urban uprisings of 1648-1650

■   The peasants' revolt led by
     Stenka Razin 1670-1671

—   The Russian frontier in 1670

0   500
|_____|
        Miles

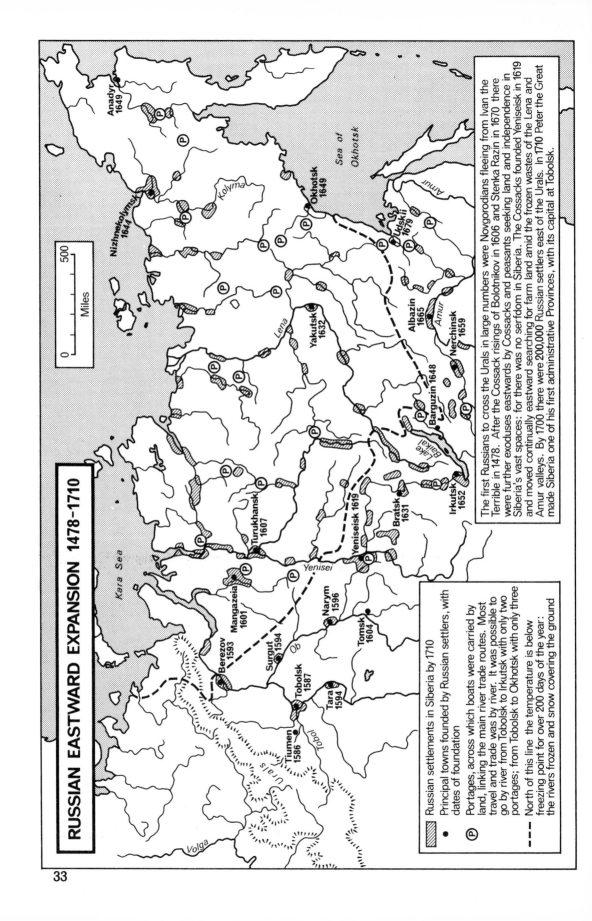

RUSSIAN EASTWARD EXPANSION 1478–1710

The first Russians to cross the Urals in large numbers were Novgorodians fleeing from Ivan the Terrible in 1478. After the Cossack risings of Bolotnikov in 1606 and Stenka Razin in 1670 there were further exoduses eastwards by Cossacks and peasants seeking land and independence in Siberia's vast spaces: for there was no serfdom in Siberia. The Cossacks founded Yeniseisk in 1619 and moved continually eastward searching for farm land amid the frozen wastes of the Lena and Amur valleys. By 1700 there were 200,000 Russian settlers east of the Urals. In 1710 Peter the Great made Siberia one of his first administrative Provinces, with its capital at Tobolsk.

Russian settlements in Siberia by 1710

● Principal towns founded by Russian settlers, with dates of foundation

Ⓟ Portages, across which boats were carried by land, linking the main river trade routes. Most travel and trade was by river. It was possible to go by river from Tobolsk to Irkutsk with only two portages; from Tobolsk to Okhotsk with only three portages.

- - - North of this line the temperature is below freezing point for over 200 days of the year: the rivers frozen and snow covering the ground

Anadyr 1649
Okhotsk 1649
Nizhnekolymsk 1644
Udskii 1679
Albazin 1665
Nerchinsk 1659
Barguzin 1648
Yakutsk 1632
Irkutsk 1652
Bratsk 1631
Yeniseisk 1619
Turukhansk 1607
Mangazeia 1601
Berezov 1593
Surgut 1594
Narym 1596
Tomsk 1604
Tobolsk 1587
Tara 1594
Tiumen 1586

Sea of Okhotsk
Kolyma
Lena
Amur
Lake Baikal
Yenisei
Kara Sea
Ob
Tobol
Urals
Volga

500
Miles
0

33

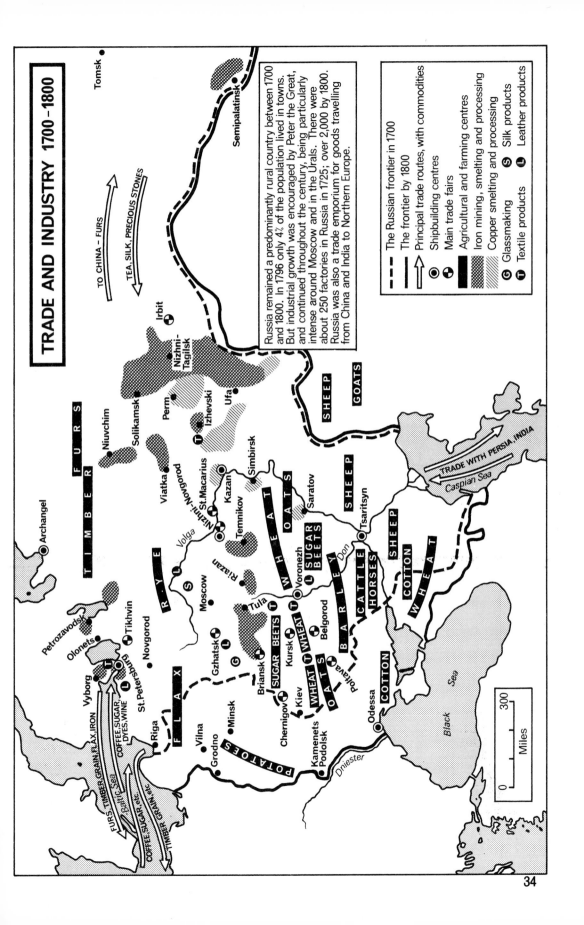

TRADE AND INDUSTRY 1700–1800

Russia remained a predominantly rural country between 1700 and 1800. In 1796 only 4% of the population lived in towns. But industrial growth was encouraged by Peter the Great, and continued throughout the century, being particularly intense around Moscow and in the Urals. There were about 250 factories in Russia in 1725; over 2,000 by 1800. Russia was also a trade emporium for goods travelling from China and India to Northern Europe.

Legend:
- The Russian frontier in 1700
- The frontier by 1800
- Principal trade routes, with commodities
- Shipbuilding centres
- Main trade fairs
- Agricultural and farming centres
- Iron mining, smelting and processing
- Copper smelting and processing
- **G** Glassmaking
- **S** Silk products
- **T** Textile products
- **L** Leather products

TO CHINA – FURS

TEA, SILK, PRECIOUS STONES

TRADE WITH PERSIA, INDIA

Caspian Sea

SHEEP
GOATS
SHEEP
SHEEP
SHEEP
COTTON
WHEAT
COTTON
CATTLE
HORSES
BARLEY
SUGAR BEETS
OATS
WHEAT
WHEAT
OATS
SUGAR BEETS
WHEAT
RYE
FLAX
POTATOES
TIMBER
FURS

Tomsk

Semipalatinsk

Irbit

Nizhni-Tagilsk

Perm
Solikamsk
Niuvchim
Izhevski
Ufa
Viatka
St. Macarius
Simbirsk
Kazan
Nizhni-Novgorod
Temnikov
Saratov
Voronezh
Tsaritsyn
Riazan
Volga
Don

Archangel

Petrozavodsk
Olonets
Tikhvin
Novgorod
Vyborg
St. Petersburg
Moscow
Tula
Gzhatsk
Briansk
Kursk
Belgorod
Kiev
Chernigov
Poltava
Minsk
Vilna
Grodno
Riga
Kamenets Podolsk
Odessa
Dniester

FURS, TIMBER, GRAIN, FLAX, IRON
COFFEE, SUGAR, DYES, WINE
COFFEE, SUGAR, etc.
TIMBER, GRAIN, etc.

Baltic Sea

Black Sea

0   300
Miles

34

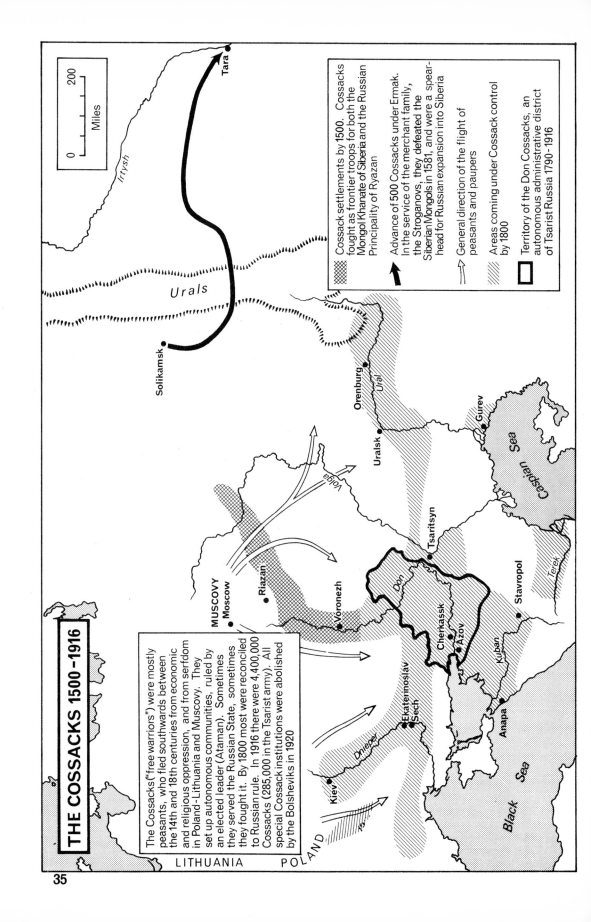

THE COSSACKS 1500-1916

The Cossacks ("free warriors") were mostly peasants, who fled southwards between the 14th and 18th centuries from economic and religious oppression, and from serfdom in Poland-Lithuania and Muscovy. They set up autonomous communities, ruled by an elected leader (Ataman). Sometimes they served the Russian State, sometimes they fought it. By 1800 most were reconciled to Russian rule. In 1916 there were 4,400,000 Cossacks (285,000 in the Tsarist army). All special Cossack institutions were abolished by the Bolsheviks in 1920

Cossack settlements by 1500. Cossacks fought as frontier troops for both the Mongol Khanate of Siberia and the Russian Principality of Ryazan

Advance of 500 Cossacks under Ermak. In the service of the merchant family, the Stroganovs, they defeated the Siberian Mongols in 1581, and were a spearhead for Russian expansion into Siberia

General direction of the flight of peasants and paupers

Areas coming under Cossack control by 1800

Territory of the Don Cossacks, an autonomous administrative district of Tsarist Russia 1790-1916

LITHUANIA

POLAND

MUSCOVY
Moscow

Riazan

Voronezh

Kiev

Ekaterinoslav
Sech

Don

Cherkassk

Azov

Kuban

Anapa

Black Sea

Volga

Uralsk

Orenburg

Ural

Tsaritsyn

Gurev

Caspian Sea

Stavropol

Terek

Solikamsk

Urals

Irtysh

Tara

Miles
0   200

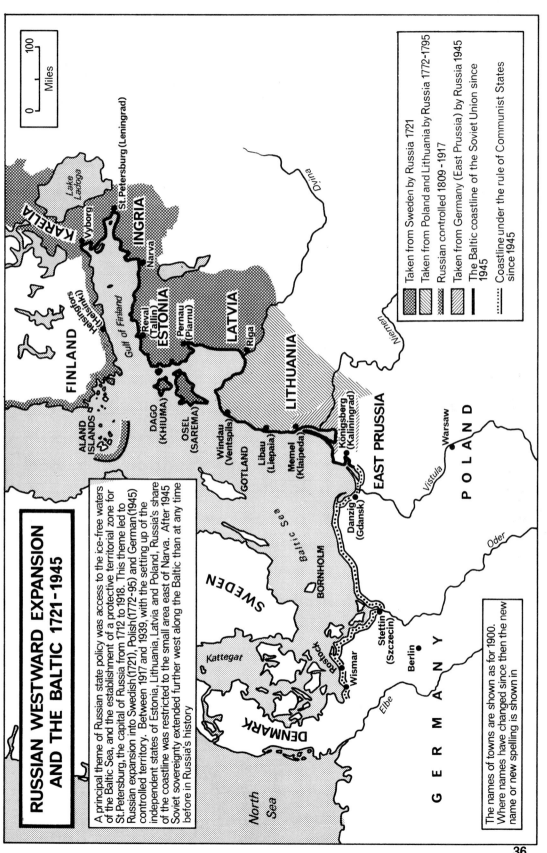

RUSSIAN WESTWARD EXPANSION AND THE BALTIC 1721-1945

A principal theme of Russian state policy was access to the ice-free waters of the Baltic Sea, and the establishment of a protective territorial zone for St.Petersburg, the capital of Russia from 1712 to 1918. This theme led to Russian expansion into Swedish (1721), Polish(1772–95) and German(1945) controlled territory. Between 1917 and 1939, with the setting up of the independent states of Estonia, Lithuania, Latvia and Poland, Russia's share of the coastline was restricted to the small area east of Narva. After 1945 Soviet sovereignty extended further west along the Baltic than at any time before in Russia's history

Legend:
- Taken from Sweden by Russia 1721
- Taken from Poland and Lithuania by Russia 1772-1795
- Russian controlled 1809 - 1917
- Taken from Germany (East Prussia) by Russia 1945
- The Baltic coastline of the Soviet Union since 1945
- Coastline under the rule of Communist States since 1945

The names of towns are shown as for 1900. Where names have changed since then the new name or new spelling is shown in

Scale: 0 — 100 Miles

Labels on map:
KARELIA, Lake Ladoga, Vyborg, St.Petersburg (Leningrad), INGRIA, Narva, FINLAND, Helsingfors (Helsinki), Gulf of Finland, Reval (Tallin), ESTONIA, Pernau (Piarnu), LATVIA, Riga, Dyina, ALAND ISLANDS, DAGO (KHIUMA), OSEL (SAREMA), Windau (Ventspils), Libau (Liepaia), GOTLAND, Memel (Klaipeda), LITHUANIA, Königsberg (Kaliningrad), EAST PRUSSIA, Niemen, Warsaw, POLAND, Vistula, Oder, Baltic Sea, BORNHOLM, Danzig (Gdansk), SWEDEN, Kattegat, Rostock, Stettin (Szczecin), Wismar, Berlin, GERMANY, Elbe, DENMARK, North Sea

36

Section Two

Imperial Russia

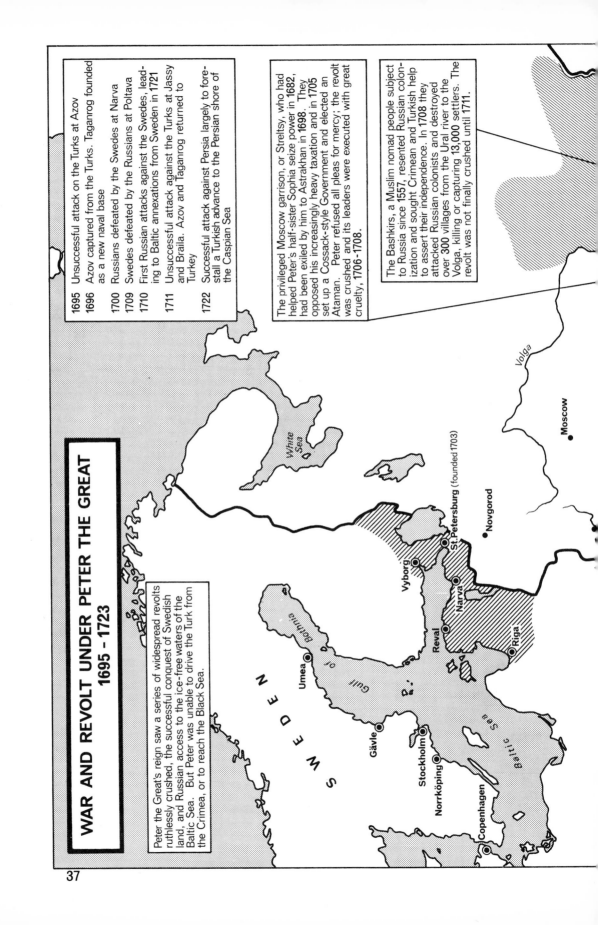

WAR AND REVOLT UNDER PETER THE GREAT
1695 – 1723

Peter the Great's reign saw a series of widespread revolts ruthlessly crushed, the successful conquest of Swedish land, and Russian access to the ice-free waters of the Baltic Sea. But Peter was unable to drive the Turk from the Crimea, or to reach the Black Sea.

1695 Unsuccessful attack on the Turks at Azov
1696 Azov captured from the Turks. Taganrog founded as a new naval base
1700 Russians defeated by the Swedes at Narva
1709 Swedes defeated by the Russians at Poltava
1710 First Russian attacks against the Swedes, leading to Baltic annexations from Sweden in 1721
1711 Unsuccessful attack against the Turks at Jassy and Braila. Azov and Taganrog returned to Turkey
1722 Successful attack against Persia largely to forestall a Turkish advance to the Persian shore of the Caspian Sea

The privileged Moscow garrison, or Streltsy, who had helped Peter's half-sister Sophia seize power in 1682, had been exiled by him to Astrakhan in 1698. They opposed his increasingly heavy taxation and in 1705 set up a Cossack-style Government and elected an Ataman. Peter refused all pleas for mercy; the revolt was crushed and its leaders were executed with great cruelty, 1706-1708.

The Bashkirs, a Muslim nomad people subject to Russia since 1557, resented Russian colonization and sought Crimean and Turkish help to assert their independence. In 1708 they attacked Russian colonists and destroyed over 300 villages from the Ural river to the Volga, killing or capturing 13,000 settlers. The revolt was not finally crushed until 1711.

White Sea

Volga

Moscow

Novgorod

St.Petersburg (founded 1703)

Vyborg

Narva

Reval

Riga

Umeå

S W E D E N

Gulf of Bothnia

Gävle

Stockholm

Norrköping

Baltic Sea

Copenhagen

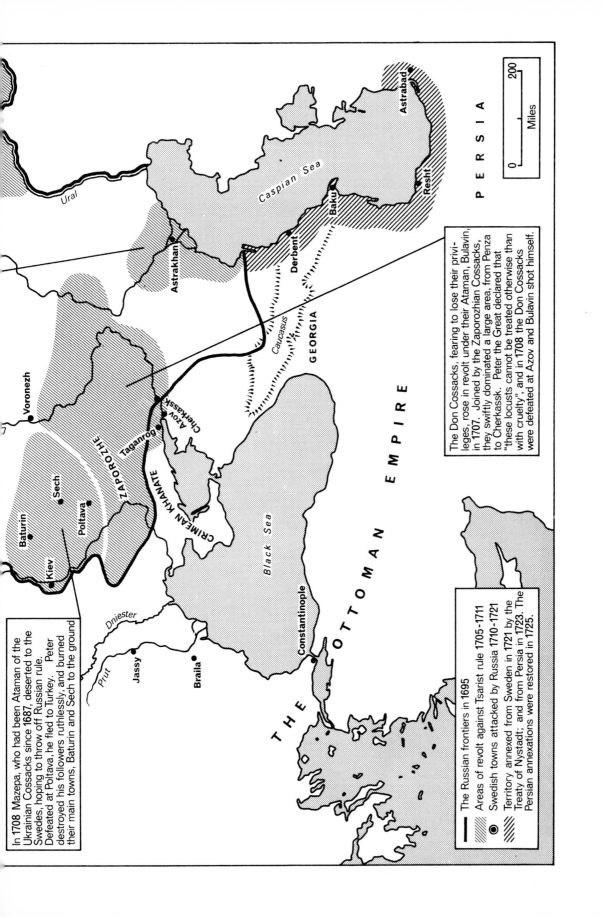

In 1708 Mazepa, who had been Ataman of the Ukrainian Cossacks since 1687, deserted to the Swedes, hoping to throw off Russian rule. Defeated at Poltava, he fled to Turkey. Peter destroyed his followers ruthlessly, and burned their main towns, Baturin and Sech to the ground

The Don Cossacks, fearing to lose their privileges, rose in revolt under their Ataman, Bulavin, in 1707. Joined by the Zaporozhian Cossacks, they swiftly dominated a large area, from Penza to Cherkassk. Peter the Great declared that "these locusts cannot be treated otherwise than with cruelty", and in 1708 the Don Cossacks were defeated at Azov and Bulavin shot himself.

The Russian frontiers in 1695

Areas of revolt against Tsarist rule 1705-1711

⊙ Swedish towns attacked by Russia 1710-1721

Territory annexed from Sweden in 1721 by the Treaty of Nystadt; and from Persia in 1723. The Persian annexations were restored in 1725.

Voronezh

Baturin
Sech
Kiev
Poltava
ZAPOROZHE
Taganrog
Azov
Cherkassk
CRIMEAN KHANATE

Dniester
Prut
Jassy
Braila

Black Sea

Constantinople

THE OTTOMAN EMPIRE

GEORGIA

Caucasus

Derbent

Baku

Resht

Astrabad

P E R S I A

Caspian Sea

Astrakhan

Ural

0   200
Miles

THE PROVINCES AND POPULATION OF RUSSIA IN 1724

0   300
Miles

St. Petersburg

Selected as the site of a new town by Peter the Great in 1703, and built at great cost in human life by serf labour, St. Petersburg became the seat of the Russian Government in 1712. Courtiers and noble families were compelled by law to live there from 1725. The city had a population of 200,000 by 1788.

White Sea

Archangel

A R C H A N G E L

Dvina

S I B E R I A

Gulf of Finland

St. Petersburg

Novgorod

Vologda

Viatka

Perm

S T. P E T E R S B U R G

Pskov

Kostroma

Tver

Moscow

Nizhni Novgorod

Volga

Kazan

K A Z A N

Smolensk

M O S C O W

Riazan

Simbirsk

Mogilev

SMOLENSK

Tula

Samara

Orel

Tambov

Penza

Orenburg

Dnieper

Chernigov

K I E V

A Z O V

Voronezh

Saratov

Ural

C O S S A C K S

Kiev

Poltava

Kharkov

Don

Dniester

Volga

C O S S A C K S

Azov

Caspian Sea

Black Sea

COSSACKS

COSSACKS

It was Peter the Great who first divided Russia into Provinces (known as "Gubernii" or "Governments"). These administrative divisions served a military, financial and judicial purpose. They enabled Peter to supervise the whole kingdom by means of Governors responsible directly to himself. Catherine the Great later divided these Provinces into smaller units. The establishment of Provincial administrations led to a rapid growth of bureaucracy, and a complex hierarchy of local seniority. The population of Russia in 1724 was just over 15 million, of whom only ½ million lived in towns.

--- Russia's frontiers by 1725

━━ Provinces established by Peter the Great

▓ Area with over 20 inhabitants in every square verst. (One verst = two-thirds of a mile)

▨ Area with between 10 and 20 inhabitants per square verst

Russian territory with less than 10 inhabitants per square verst is not shaded

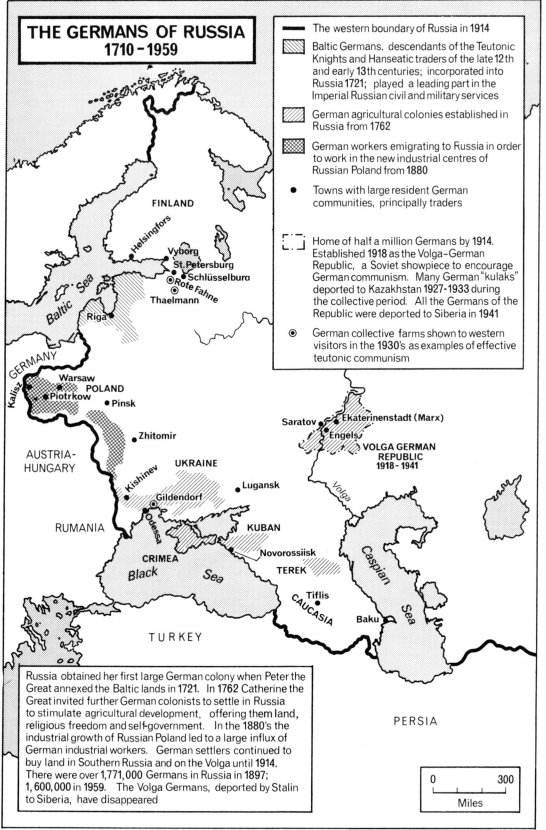

THE GERMANS OF RUSSIA
1710 - 1959

—— The western boundary of Russia in 1914

Baltic Germans, descendants of the Teutonic Knights and Hanseatic traders of the late 12th and early 13th centuries; incorporated into Russia 1721; played a leading part in the Imperial Russian civil and military services

German agricultural colonies established in Russia from 1762

German workers emigrating to Russia in order to work in the new industrial centres of Russian Poland from 1880

● Towns with large resident German communities, principally traders

Home of half a million Germans by 1914. Established 1918 as the Volga-German Republic, a Soviet showpiece to encourage German communism. Many German "kulaks" deported to Kazakhstan 1927-1933 during the collective period. All the Germans of the Republic were deported to Siberia in 1941

◉ German collective farms shown to western visitors in the 1930's as examples of effective teutonic communism

FINLAND

Helsingfors

Vyborg
St.Petersburg
● Schlüsselburg
◉ Rote Fahne
Thaelmann

Baltic Sea

Riga ●

GERMANY

Warsaw ●
POLAND
● Piotrkow
Kalisz ●

● Pinsk

AUSTRIA-
HUNGARY

● Zhitomir

Kishinev ●

UKRAINE

Gildendorf ◉

Odessa ●

Saratov ● ● Ekaterinenstadt (Marx)
● Engels
VOLGA GERMAN
REPUBLIC
1918-1941

● Lugansk

Volga

KUBAN

Novorossiisk ●

CRIMEA
Black Sea

TEREK

Tiflis ●
CAUCASIA

Baku ●

Caspian Sea

RUMANIA

TURKEY

PERSIA

Russia obtained her first large German colony when Peter the Great annexed the Baltic lands in 1721. In 1762 Catherine the Great invited further German colonists to settle in Russia to stimulate agricultural development, offering them land, religious freedom and self-government. In the 1880's the industrial growth of Russian Poland led to a large influx of German industrial workers. German settlers continued to buy land in Southern Russia and on the Volga until 1914. There were over 1,771,000 Germans in Russia in 1897; 1,600,000 in 1959. The Volga Germans, deported by Stalin to Siberia, have disappeared

0   300
|————————|
Miles

THE EXPANSION OF CHINA 1720–1760

THE

RUSSIAN

EMPIRE

Okhotsk⊙

Yakutsk⊙

Tobolsk⊙

Yeniseisk⊙

Albazin

Tomsk⊙   Krasnoyarsk⊙

Omsk⊙   Nerchinsk⊙

                    Irkutsk⊙   Lake
                                      Baikal   Harbin

Semipalatinsk⊙
              Ustkamenogorsk   Maimachin
        ⊙
                                      M O N G O L S

              Lake
              Balkhash   Peking
        Kulja   Hami
              Urumchi   Nanking

Yarkand   Sian
        DOMINIONS OF THE
        ZUNGAR KALMUKS   C H I N A

Khotan   Chengtu

                    T I B E T   Canton
              Lhasa
        Himalayas   Yunnan

⊙	Cities founded by the Russians before 1720
■	The Chinese Empire in 1720, ruled by the Manchu Dynasty
▨	Under Chinese control by 1720, providing the Manchus with a reservoir of military power
▨	Conquered by China between 1724 and 1764
▨	Conquered by China in 1780

0   500
Miles

RUSSIAN EXPANSION UNDER CATHERINE THE GREAT 1762-1796

The Provinces of Russia in 1750

Territory annexed by Russia 1762-1796, giving Russia an outlet on the Black Sea, and a common frontier with Prussia and Austria

White Sea

Archangel
ARCHANGEL

FINLAND

Helsingfors

Baltic Sea

ESTONIA
LIVONIA
ST. PETERSBURG

Novgorod
NOVGOROD

Vologda

Viatka

Perm

KAZAN

Kazan

Ufa

UFA

KURLAND

Pskov

Tver

MOSCOW
Moscow

PRUSSIA

Niemen

Vilna
LITHUANIA
Minsk
WHITE
RUSSIA
Pinsk

SMOLENSK

NIZHNI
NOVGOROD

Stavropol
Samara

Warsaw

AUSTRIA

PODLESIA
Lutsk

KIEV
Kiev

Orel

BELGOROD

VORONEZH

Belgorod

Dnieper

ASTRAKHAN

Dniester

PODOLIA

ZAPOROZHE

Jassy

Odessa
Taganrog

Astrakhan

Kutchuk
Kainardji

Sebastopol
CRIMEA
KUBAN

KABARDA

Tarki

Caspian Sea

THE OTTOMAN EMPIRE

Black Sea

Constantinople

Kars

0   200
Miles

PERSIA

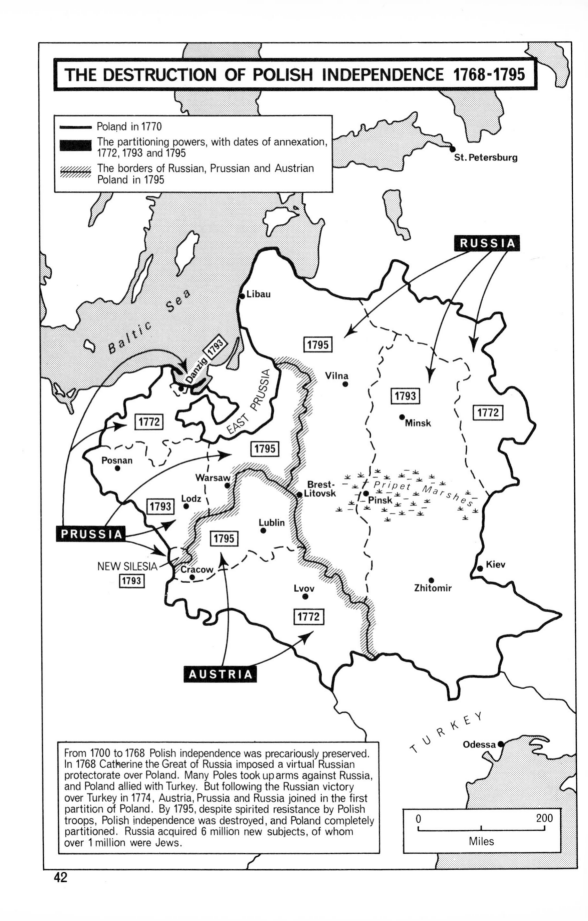

THE DESTRUCTION OF POLISH INDEPENDENCE 1768-1795

Poland in 1770

The partitioning powers, with dates of annexation, 1772, 1793 and 1795

The borders of Russian, Prussian and Austrian Poland in 1795

St. Petersburg

RUSSIA

Baltic Sea

Libau

1795

Danzig 1793

EAST PRUSSIA

Vilna

1793

1772

1772

Posnan

1795

Minsk

Warsaw

Brest-Litovsk

Pripet Marshes

1793

Lodz

Pinsk

Lublin

PRUSSIA

1795

Kiev

NEW SILESIA

Cracow

1793

Lvov

Zhitomir

1772

AUSTRIA

TURKEY

Odessa

From 1700 to 1768 Polish independence was precariously preserved. In 1768 Catherine the Great of Russia imposed a virtual Russian protectorate over Poland. Many Poles took up arms against Russia, and Poland allied with Turkey. But following the Russian victory over Turkey in 1774, Austria, Prussia and Russia joined in the first partition of Poland. By 1795, despite spirited resistance by Polish troops, Polish independence was destroyed, and Poland completely partitioned. Russia acquired 6 million new subjects, of whom over 1 million were Jews.

0   200

Miles

THE RUSSIAN ANNEXATIONS OF POLAND 1772-1795

Baltic Sea

LATVIA

Pskov

0   150
Miles

Windau

Riga

Libau

Mitau

Palanga

Dvinsk

Nevel

Memel

LITHUANIA

Dvina

Polotsk

Königsberg

Kovno

1795

Vitebsk

Smolensk

Vilna

1793

1772

Orsha

EAST
PRUSSIA

Suvalki

Troki

Lida

Borisov

Mogilev

Mstislav

Grodno

Minsk

WHITE

Dnieper

Novogrudok

Vilkoviski

Mir

RUSSIA

Bobruisk

Bialystok

Baranovichi

Slutsk

Gomel

Starodub

Warsaw

Brest-Litovsk

Pinsk

Pripet

Marshes

Turov

Mozyr

Pripet

Lublin

Kovel

Olevsk

Chernigov

AUSTRIAN-ANNEXED

POLAND

VOLHYNIA

Lutsk

WESTERN

UKRAINE

UKRAINE

Rovno

Zhitomir

Kiev

Dubno

Pereyaslavl

GALICIA

Lvov

Staro-
Konstantinov

Berdychev

Przemysl

Tarnopol

Boguslav

Dnieper

Vinnitsa

PODOLIA

Stanislavov

Kamenets-
Podolsk

Bug

AUSTRIA

BESSARABIA

Dniester

Balta

RUSSIAN-
ANNEXED

TURKEY

Kherson

Dnieper

TURKEY

1791
Odessa

1774

Black
Sea

Legend:
- The western part of Russia in 1770
- Partition lines
- Principal Polish military resistance to the Russians
- The western frontier of Russia 1795

PRUSSIAN-ANNEXED POLAND

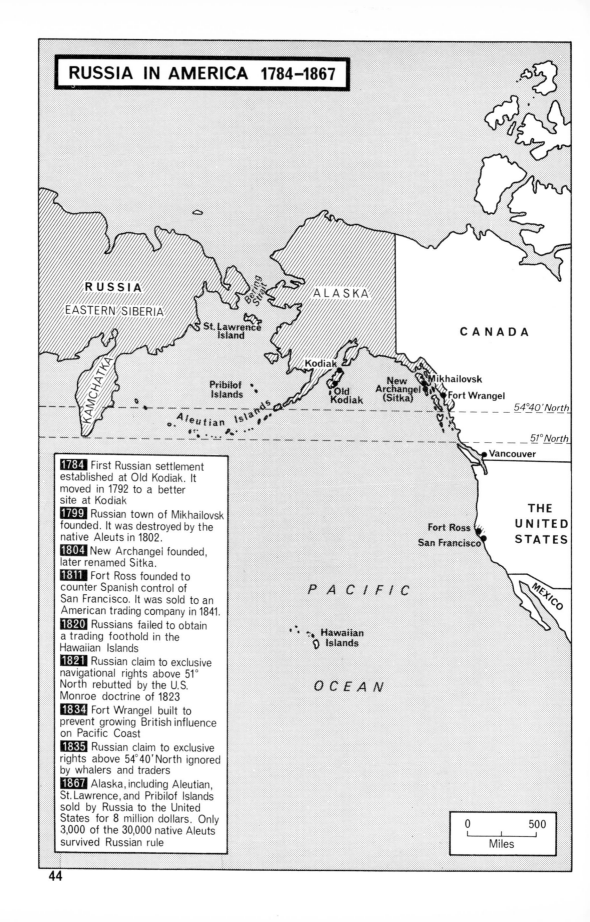

RUSSIA IN AMERICA 1784–1867

RUSSIA

EASTERN SIBERIA

KAMCHATKA

Bering Strait

St. Lawrence Island

ALASKA

CANADA

Kodiak

Pribilof Islands

Old Kodiak

New Archangel (Sitka)

Mikhailovsk

Fort Wrangel

54°40' North

Aleutian Islands

51° North

Vancouver

THE UNITED STATES

Fort Ross
San Francisco

PACIFIC

MEXICO

Hawaiian Islands

OCEAN

1784 First Russian settlement established at Old Kodiak. It moved in 1792 to a better site at Kodiak

1799 Russian town of Mikhailovsk founded. It was destroyed by the native Aleuts in 1802.

1804 New Archangel founded, later renamed Sitka.

1811 Fort Ross founded to counter Spanish control of San Francisco. It was sold to an American trading company in 1841.

1820 Russians failed to obtain a trading foothold in the Hawaiian Islands

1821 Russian claim to exclusive navigational rights above 51° North rebutted by the U.S. Monroe doctrine of 1823

1834 Fort Wrangel built to prevent growing British influence on Pacific Coast

1835 Russian claim to exclusive rights above 54°40' North ignored by whalers and traders

1867 Alaska, including Aleutian, St. Lawrence, and Pribilof Islands sold by Russia to the United States for 8 million dollars. Only 3,000 of the 30,000 native Aleuts survived Russian rule

0   500
Miles

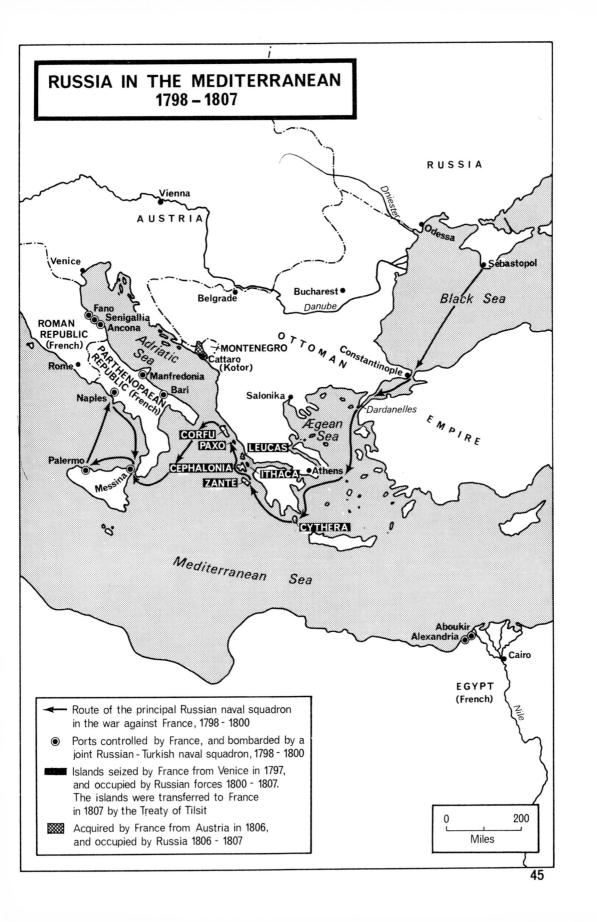

RUSSIA IN THE MEDITERRANEAN
1798 – 1807

RUSSIA

Vienna

AUSTRIA

Dniester

Odessa

Venice

Sebastopol

Belgrade

Bucharest

Black Sea

Danube

Fano
Senigallia
Ancona

ROMAN
REPUBLIC
(French)

Adriatic
Sea

OTTOMAN

Constantinople

MONTENEGRO
Cattaro
(Kotor)

Rome

PARTHENOPAEAN
REPUBLIC
(French)

Manfredonia
Bari

Salonika

Dardanelles

EMPIRE

Naples

Ægean
Sea

Palermo

CORFU
PAXO

LEUCAS

Athens

Messina

CEPHALONIA
ZANTE

ITHACA

CYTHERA

Mediterranean   Sea

Aboukir
Alexandria

Cairo

EGYPT
(French)

Nile

→ Route of the principal Russian naval squadron
in the war against France, 1798 - 1800

⊚ Ports controlled by France, and bombarded by a
joint Russian - Turkish naval squadron, 1798 - 1800

▬ Islands seized by France from Venice in 1797,
and occupied by Russian forces 1800 - 1807.
The islands were transferred to France
in 1807 by the Treaty of Tilsit

▨ Acquired by France from Austria in 1806,
and occupied by Russia 1806 - 1807

0   200
Miles

RUSSIA AND TURKEY 1721-1829

The Turks are falling like skittles, but, thank God, our men stand fast, though headless
RUSSIAN SOLDIERS' SAYING

Kiev

Dnieper

Khotin
1788

Uman
1738

Bug

Dniester

Prut

Kishinev
1739

B E S S A R A B I A

Jassy
1806

Bendery
1770

Ochakov
1788

Riabaya
Mogila
1770

Perekop

1790

Belgrade

1789
1770, 1806

Fokshani

Braila
1806

Kilia
1791

Ismail
1791, 1806

1788

Bakhchisara
1736

Negotin
1810

Craiova
1807, 1828

Bucharest
1770, 1806,
1828

Vidin
1811, 1828

Danube

Rushchuk

Silistria
1810,

1828

Kustenje
1809

Nikopol
1829

1771
1811

1774, 1828

Mangalia
1810, 1828

Kutchuk
Kainardji

1774

Turnovo
1810

Shumla
1810

1829

Varna
1810

1791

B l a c k

T U R K E Y   I N   E U R O P E

Adrianople
1829

Midia
1829

Bosphorus

Enos
1829

Corlu
1829

Constantinople

The Straits

Dardanelles

Aegean Sea

T U R K E Y

THE BLACK SEA AND THE STRAITS

1739 Treaty of Belgrade: Russian ships not allowed
into the Sea of Azov or the Black Sea

1774 Treaty of Kutchuk Kainardji: Russian merchant
ships gained the right to navigate the Black
Sea and pass the Straits; but cargoes could
be requisitioned at will

1829 Treaty of Adrianople: Russia obtained the
right of unhindered passage of unarmed ships

0   100

Miles

46

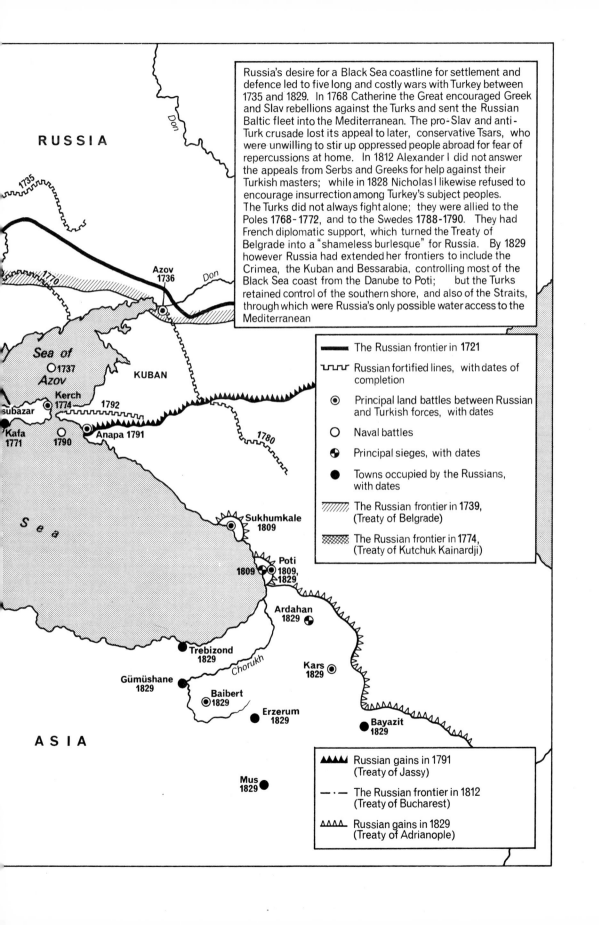

RUSSIA

Russia's desire for a Black Sea coastline for settlement and defence led to five long and costly wars with Turkey between 1735 and 1829. In 1768 Catherine the Great encouraged Greek and Slav rebellions against the Turks and sent the Russian Baltic fleet into the Mediterranean. The pro-Slav and anti-Turk crusade lost its appeal to later, conservative Tsars, who were unwilling to stir up oppressed people abroad for fear of repercussions at home. In 1812 Alexander I did not answer the appeals from Serbs and Greeks for help against their Turkish masters; while in 1828 Nicholas I likewise refused to encourage insurrection among Turkey's subject peoples. The Turks did not always fight alone; they were allied to the Poles 1768-1772, and to the Swedes 1788-1790. They had French diplomatic support, which turned the Treaty of Belgrade into a "shameless burlesque" for Russia. By 1829 however Russia had extended her frontiers to include the Crimea, the Kuban and Bessarabia, controlling most of the Black Sea coast from the Danube to Poti; but the Turks retained control of the southern shore, and also of the Straits, through which were Russia's only possible water access to the Mediterranean

1735

Azov
1736

Don

Don

Azov
1736

Sea of
Azov   ○1737

KUBAN

Kerch
1774   1792

Kafa
1771   1790   Anapa 1791

1780

S e a

Sukhumkale
1809

Poti
1809   1809,
         1829

Ardahan
1829

Trebizond
1829

Chorukh   Kars
                1829

Gümüshane
1829   Baibert
            1829

         Erzerum
         1829   Bayazit
                                 1829

ASIA

Mus
1829

	The Russian frontier in 1721
⌐⌐⌐	Russian fortified lines, with dates of completion
⊙	Principal land battles between Russian and Turkish forces, with dates
○	Naval battles
◕	Principal sieges, with dates
●	Towns occupied by the Russians, with dates
/////	The Russian frontier in 1739, (Treaty of Belgrade)
▒▒▒	The Russian frontier in 1774, (Treaty of Kutchuk Kainardji)

▲▲▲▲	Russian gains in 1791 (Treaty of Jassy)
—·—	The Russian frontier in 1812 (Treaty of Bucharest)
△△△△	Russian gains in 1829 (Treaty of Adrianople)

RUSSIA AND SWEDEN 1700-1809

From 1621 Sweden controlled the Baltic Sea and the Gulfs of Finland and Bothnia. In 1700 Peter the Great allied Russia with Poland and Denmark, in 1714 with Prussia and Hanover. His first conquest was Ingria, giving Russia a small but valued outlet on the Baltic. After several defeats, the Russians finally broke Sweden's dominance in 1721. Russia's annexation of Finland in 1809 further extended her control of the Baltic.

0 — 300 Miles

LAPLAND

Tornea

Uleaborg

Vasa

Gulf of Bothnia

FINLAND

Helsingfors

KARELIA

Kexholm

Nystad
Abo

Vyborg

Nöteborg
St. Petersburg

ALAND IS.

Gulf of Finland

Narva

INGRIA

Ivangorod

Novgorod

Stockholm

DAGÖ

Reval

ESTLAND

S W E D E N

ÖSEL

Dorpat

Pskov

GOTLAND

LIVLAND

Baltic Sea

Riga

DENMARK

Copenhagen

Stralsund

BORNHOLM

POLAND

SWEDISH POMERANIA

Stettin

HANOVER

PRUSSIA

— Sweden in 1700

■ Swedish territory conquered by Peter the Great during the Great Northern War 1700-1721, and annexed to Russia at the Treaty of Nystad 1721

Conquered by Russia, 1743

Swedish territory conquered by Alexander I and annexed to Russia in 1809

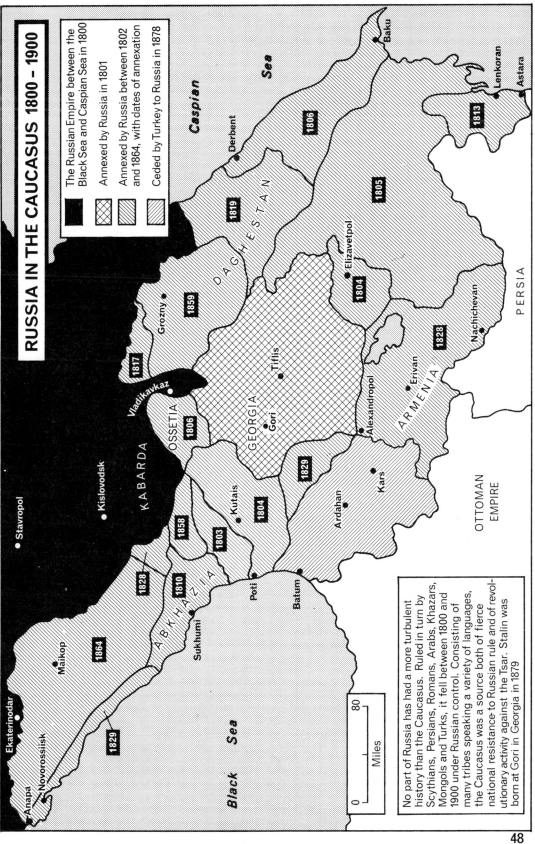

RUSSIA IN THE CAUCASUS 1800 – 1900

The Russian Empire between the Black Sea and Caspian Sea in 1800

Annexed by Russia in 1801

Annexed by Russia between 1802 and 1864, with dates of annexation

Ceded by Turkey to Russia in 1878

Caspian *Sea*

Baku

Lenkoran

Astara

1813

Derbent

1806

1805

PERSIA

DAGHESTAN

1819

1859

Grozny

Elizavetpol

1804

Nachichevan

ARMENIA

1828

Vladikavkaz

OSSETIA

1817

1806

Tiflis

GEORGIA

Gori

Erivan

Alexandropol

1829

Kars

OTTOMAN EMPIRE

KABARDA

Kislovodsk

Stavropol

Kutais

1804

Ardahan

1858

1803

ABKHAZIA

Poti

Batum

1828

1810

Sukhumi

Ekaterinodar

Novorossiisk

Maikop

1864

Anapa

1829

Black *Sea*

80

Miles

0

No part of Russia has had a more turbulent history than the Caucasus. Ruled in turn by Scythians, Persians, Romans, Arabs, Khazars, Mongols and Turks, it fell between 1800 and 1900 under Russian control. Consisting of many tribes speaking a variety of languages, the Caucasus was a source both of fierce national resistance to Russian rule and of revolutionary activity against the Tsar. Stalin was born at Gori in Georgia in 1879

48

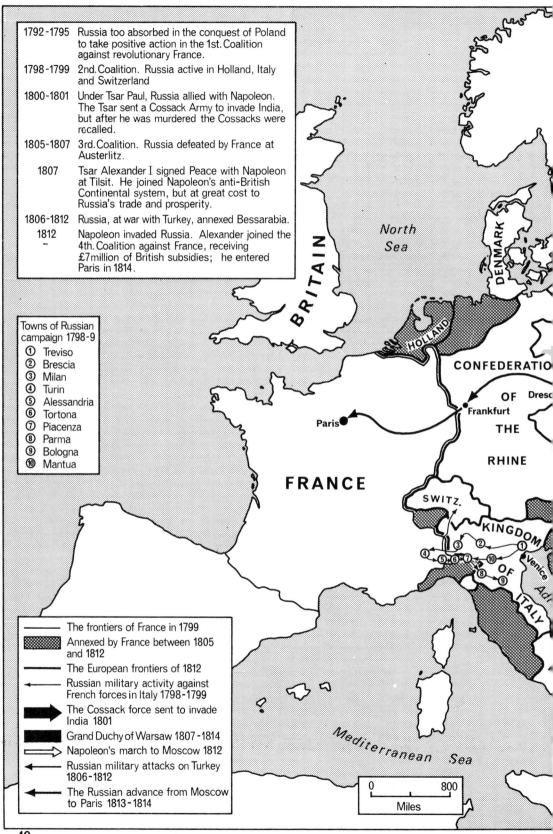

1792-1795 Russia too absorbed in the conquest of Poland to take positive action in the 1st. Coalition against revolutionary France.

1798-1799 2nd. Coalition. Russia active in Holland, Italy and Switzerland

1800-1801 Under Tsar Paul, Russia allied with Napoleon. The Tsar sent a Cossack Army to invade India, but after he was murdered the Cossacks were recalled.

1805-1807 3rd. Coalition. Russia defeated by France at Austerlitz.

1807 Tsar Alexander I signed Peace with Napoleon at Tilsit. He joined Napoleon's anti-British Continental system, but at great cost to Russia's trade and prosperity.

1806-1812 Russia, at war with Turkey, annexed Bessarabia.

1812 Napoleon invaded Russia. Alexander joined the 4th. Coalition against France, receiving £7 million of British subsidies; he entered Paris in 1814.

Towns of Russian campaign 1798-9
① Treviso
② Brescia
③ Milan
④ Turin
⑤ Alessandria
⑥ Tortona
⑦ Piacenza
⑧ Parma
⑨ Bologna
⑩ Mantua

North Sea

BRITAIN

DENMARK

HOLLAND

CONFEDERATIO
OF Dresc
Frankfurt
THE
RHINE

Paris

FRANCE

SWITZ.

KINGDOM

OF

ITALY

Venice

Adr

Mediterranean Sea

——— The frontiers of France in 1799

▓ Annexed by France between 1805 and 1812

——— The European frontiers of 1812

◄— Russian military activity against French forces in Italy 1798-1799

◄█ The Cossack force sent to invade India 1801

█ Grand Duchy of Warsaw 1807-1814

⇨ Napoleon's march to Moscow 1812

◄— Russian military attacks on Turkey 1806-1812

◄█ The Russian advance from Moscow to Paris 1813-1814

0   800
Miles

RUSSIA AND EUROPE 1789-1815

R U S S I A

Tver

Moscow

Borodino

Viazma

Riga

Riazan

Tilsit

Smolensk

Tula

Borisov

Baltic Sea

USSIA

GRAND
DUCHY
OF WARSAW

Kalisz

Napoleon championed Polish independence, and many Polish emigres joined him after 1795. In 1807 he established a Grand Duchy of Warsaw, entirely out of Prussian and Austrian Poland. The Russians planned to crush this new state, but to forestall them Napoleon marched to Moscow in 1812. 85.000 Poles served in his army. After his defeat most of the Grand Duchy was transferred to Russia, giving Russia a further 3 million Polish and 300,000 Jewish citizens.

Austerlitz

Vienna

AUSTRIA

Jassy

BESS-ARABIA

Ismail

RUMANIANS

Bucharest

Black Sea

CROATS

Iasika

Varna

SERBS

Tirnovo

Shumla

BULGARS

TURKEY IN EUROPE

GREEKS

TURKEY IN ASIA

Balkan peoples under Turkish rule, whom Alexander planned to enlist in an anti-French crusade in return for helping them obtain independence from Turkey. The plan failed.

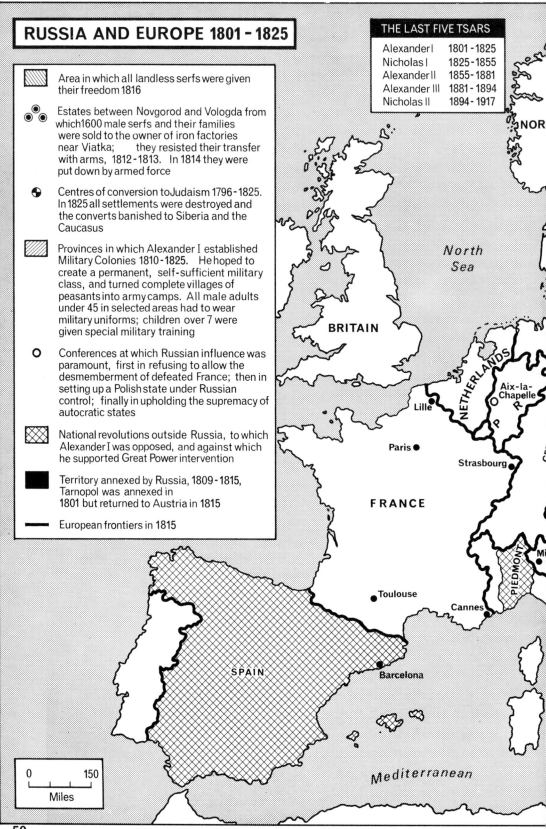

RUSSIA AND EUROPE 1801 - 1825

THE LAST FIVE TSARS	
Alexander I	1801 - 1825
Nicholas I	1825 - 1855
Alexander II	1855 - 1881
Alexander III	1881 - 1894
Nicholas II	1894 - 1917

Area in which all landless serfs were given their freedom 1816

Estates between Novgorod and Vologda from which 1600 male serfs and their families were sold to the owner of iron factories near Viatka; they resisted their transfer with arms, 1812-1813. In 1814 they were put down by armed force

Centres of conversion to Judaism 1796-1825. In 1825 all settlements were destroyed and the converts banished to Siberia and the Caucasus

Provinces in which Alexander I established Military Colonies 1810-1825. He hoped to create a permanent, self-sufficient military class, and turned complete villages of peasants into army camps. All male adults under 45 in selected areas had to wear military uniforms; children over 7 were given special military training

Conferences at which Russian influence was paramount, first in refusing to allow the desmemberment of defeated France; then in setting up a Polish state under Russian control; finally in upholding the supremacy of autocratic states

National revolutions outside Russia, to which Alexander I was opposed, and against which he supported Great Power intervention

Territory annexed by Russia, 1809-1815, Tarnopol was annexed in 1801 but returned to Austria in 1815

European frontiers in 1815

NOR

North
Sea

BRITAIN

NETHERLANDS

Aix-la-Chapelle

Lille

Paris

Strasbourg

FRANCE

Toulouse

Cannes

PIEDMONT

Mi

SPAIN

Barcelona

Mediterranean

0   150
Miles

50

FINLAND

ALAND
ISLANDS

SWEDEN

Viatka ●

● Vologda

St.
Petersburg ●

Novgorod ●

Baltic Sea

● Moscow

RUSSIA

Tula ◒

Saratov ◓

Mogilev ●

Bobrov ◓

Pavlovsk ◓

Carlsbad

Prague   Troppau

Lemberg ●
Tarnopol ●

POLAND

BESSARABIA

Ekaterinoslav ●

Vienna

AUSTRIA–
HUNGARY

Nikolaev ●

Laibach

Bucharest ●

Black Sea

Belgrade

T   U

R

NAPLES

Cattaro

Naples

Constantinople ●   K   E   Y

GREECE

Athens

Sea

Like Catherine the Great on her accession,
Alexander I was looked to on his accession
(in 1801) as a potential source of liberal-
ization. In the war against Napoleon he acted
as the enemy of tyrants and friend of the
oppressed. But by 1820 he had become a
pillar of autocracy both in Russia and
abroad. Under Alexander, Russia's western
frontier reached its furthest western extent,
and from 1820 to 1917 it was unchanged

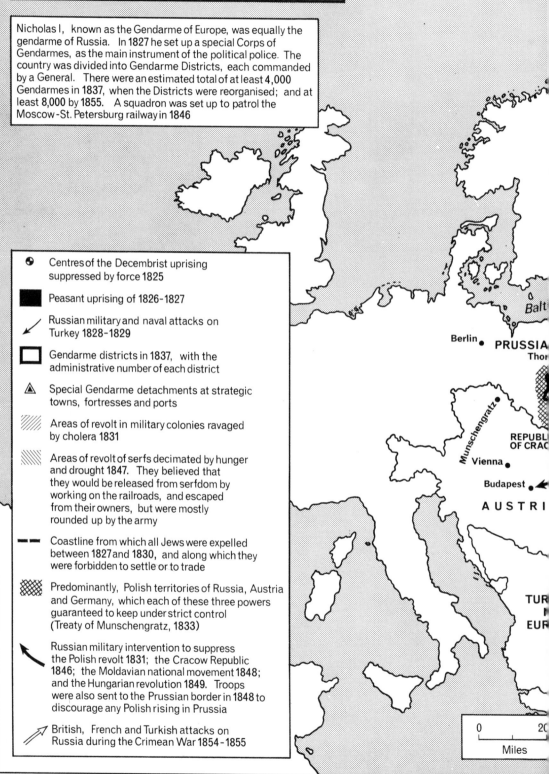

RUSSIA UNDER NICHOLAS I 1825-1855

Nicholas I, known as the Gendarme of Europe, was equally the gendarme of Russia. In 1827 he set up a special Corps of Gendarmes, as the main instrument of the political police. The country was divided into Gendarme Districts, each commanded by a General. There were an estimated total of at least 4,000 Gendarmes in 1837, when the Districts were reorganised; and at least 8,000 by 1855. A squadron was set up to patrol the Moscow-St. Petersburg railway in 1846

Centres of the Decembrist uprising suppressed by force 1825

Peasant uprising of 1826-1827

Russian military and naval attacks on Turkey 1828-1829

Gendarme districts in 1837, with the administrative number of each district

Special Gendarme detachments at strategic towns, fortresses and ports

Areas of revolt in military colonies ravaged by cholera 1831

Areas of revolt of serfs decimated by hunger and drought 1847. They believed that they would be released from serfdom by working on the railroads, and escaped from their owners, but were mostly rounded up by the army

Coastline from which all Jews were expelled between 1827 and 1830, and along which they were forbidden to settle or to trade

Predominantly, Polish territories of Russia, Austria and Germany, which each of these three powers guaranteed to keep under strict control (Treaty of Munschengratz, 1833)

Russian military intervention to suppress the Polish revolt 1831; the Cracow Republic 1846; the Moldavian national movement 1848; and the Hungarian revolution 1849. Troops were also sent to the Prussian border in 1848 to discourage any Polish rising in Prussia

British, French and Turkish attacks on Russia during the Crimean War 1854-1855

Berlin
PRUSSIA
Thor

Balt

Munschengratz

REPUBL
OF CRAC

Vienna

Budapest

AUSTRI

TUR

EUR

0   20
Miles

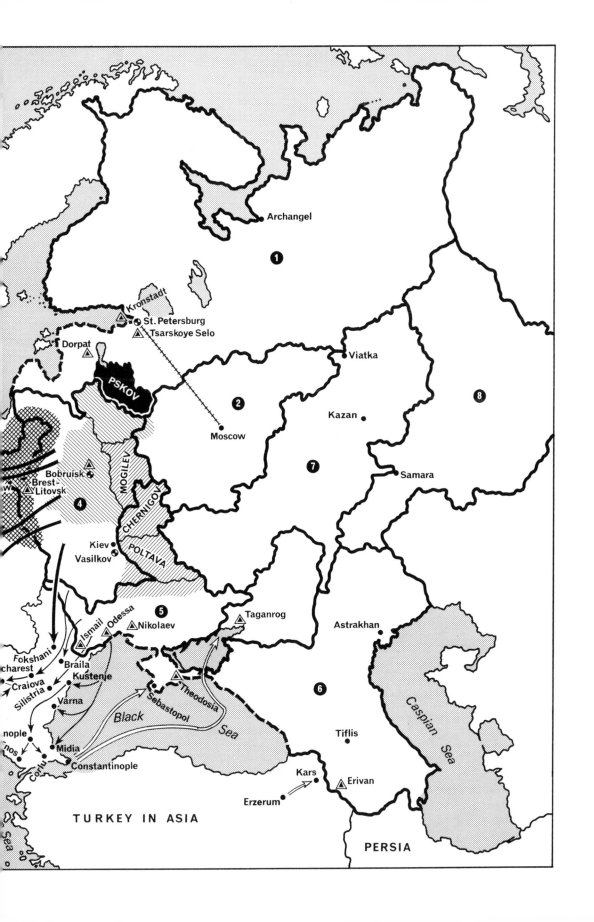

Archangel

①

Kronstadt
△ ⊕ St. Petersburg
△ Tsarskoye Selo
Dorpat ▲

Viatka ●

PSKOV

②

Kazan ●

⑧

MOGILEV

Bobruisk ⊕
Brest- ▲
Litovsk ▲

④

CHERNIGOV

⑦

Samara ●

Kiev ●
Vasilkov ⊕

POLTAVA

⑤

△ Odessa
Ismail ▲ △ Nikolaev

△ Taganrog

Astrakhan ●

Fokshani
charest ●
Braila ●
Kustenje ●
Craiova ●
Silistria ●
Varna ●

⑥

nople ●
nos ●
Midia ●
Constantinople

Black Sea

Sebastopol
△ Theodosia

Tiflis ●

Caspian Sea

Corfu

Kars
Erzerum

△ Erivan

TURKEY IN ASIA

PERSIA

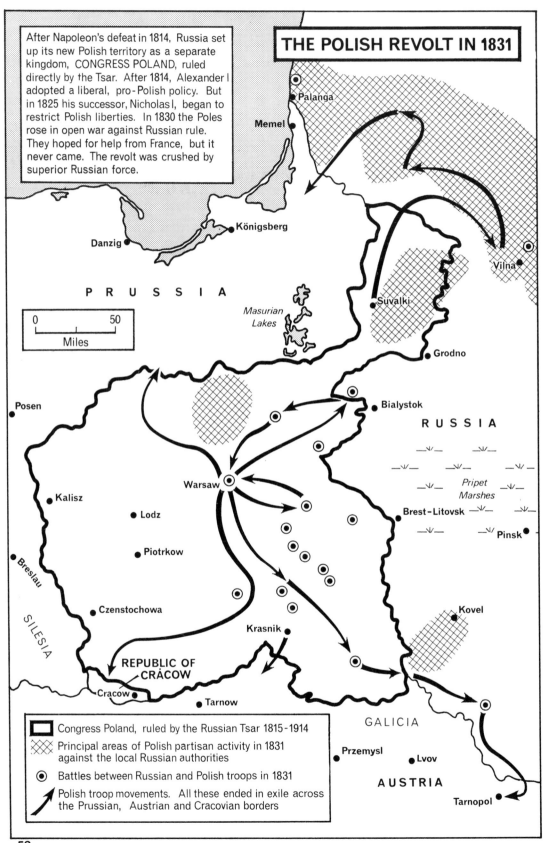

THE POLISH REVOLT IN 1831

After Napoleon's defeat in 1814, Russia set up its new Polish territory as a separate kingdom, CONGRESS POLAND, ruled directly by the Tsar. After 1814, Alexander I adopted a liberal, pro-Polish policy. But in 1825 his successor, Nicholas I, began to restrict Polish liberties. In 1830 the Poles rose in open war against Russian rule. They hoped for help from France, but it never came. The revolt was crushed by superior Russian force.

Palanga

Memel

Königsberg

Danzig

P R U S S I A

Masurian Lakes

Vilna

Suvalki

0   50
Miles

Grodno

Posen

R U S S I A

Bialystok

Pripet Marshes

Warsaw

Kalisz

Lodz

Brest-Litovsk

Pinsk

Piotrkow

Breslau

Kovel

SILESIA

Czenstochowa

Krasnik

REPUBLIC OF CRACOW

Cracow

Tarnow

GALICIA

Przemysl

Lvov

AUSTRIA

Tarnopol

Congress Poland, ruled by the Russian Tsar 1815-1914

Principal areas of Polish partisan activity in 1831 against the local Russian authorities

Battles between Russian and Polish troops in 1831

Polish troop movements. All these ended in exile across the Prussian, Austrian and Cracovian borders

52

THE POLISH REVOLT IN 1861

The Polish rising of 1831 was largely the work of the Polish aristocracy and land-owners. But by 1860 discontent against Russian rule had spread to the middle classes and intelligentsia. The revolt of 1861 took place throughout Congress Poland. It was crushed after three years of bitter fighting, during which time the Russians had to call in Austrian and Prussian military help

0 — 50
Miles

Memel

Königsberg

Danzig

Kovno

Vilna

Troki

PRUSSIA

Masurian Lakes

Mlava

Bialystok

RUSSIA

Warsaw

Pripet

Kalisz

Marshes

Radomsk

Lublin

Kovel

Czenstochowa

Krasnik

Zamosc

Cracow

Tarnow

Brody

Lvov

Przemysl

AUSTRIA

Congress Poland, ruled by the Russian Tsar 1815 - 1914

○   Centres of the Polish revolt 1861 - 1863

Prussian and Austrian troops helping Russia to suppress the uprising

⊙   Principal battles

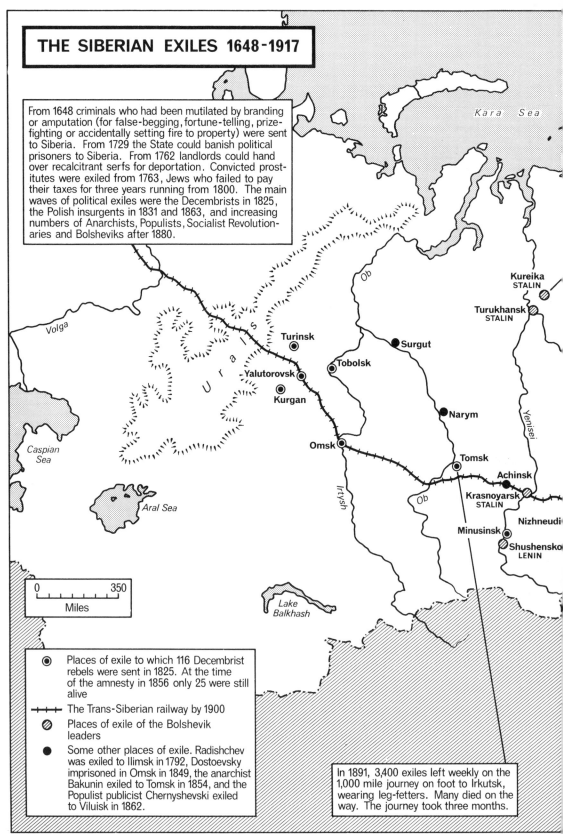

THE SIBERIAN EXILES 1648-1917

From 1648 criminals who had been mutilated by branding or amputation (for false-begging, fortune-telling, prize-fighting or accidentally setting fire to property) were sent to Siberia. From 1729 the State could banish political prisoners to Siberia. From 1762 landlords could hand over recalcitrant serfs for deportation. Convicted prostitutes were exiled from 1763, Jews who failed to pay their taxes for three years running from 1800. The main waves of political exiles were the Decembrists in 1825, the Polish insurgents in 1831 and 1863, and increasing numbers of Anarchists, Populists, Socialist Revolutionaries and Bolsheviks after 1880.

Kara Sea

Volga

Caspian Sea

Aral Sea

U r a l s

Ob

Kureika
STALIN

Turukhansk
STALIN

Turinsk

Surgut

Tobolsk

Yalutorovsk

Kurgan

Narym

Yenisei

Omsk

Irtysh

Ob

Tomsk

Achinsk

Krasnoyarsk
STALIN

Nizhneudi

Minusinsk

Shushensko
LENIN

Lake Balkhash

```
0          350
|__|__|__|__|
    Miles
```

⊙ Places of exile to which 116 Decembrist rebels were sent in 1825. At the time of the amnesty in 1856 only 25 were still alive

+++ The Trans-Siberian railway by 1900

⊘ Places of exile of the Bolshevik leaders

● Some other places of exile. Radishchev was exiled to Ilimsk in 1792, Dostoevsky imprisoned in Omsk in 1849, the anarchist Bakunin exiled to Tomsk in 1854, and the Populist publicist Chernyshevski exiled to Viluisk in 1862.

In 1891, 3,400 exiles left weekly on the 1,000 mile journey on foot to Irkutsk, wearing leg-fetters. Many died on the way. The journey took three months.

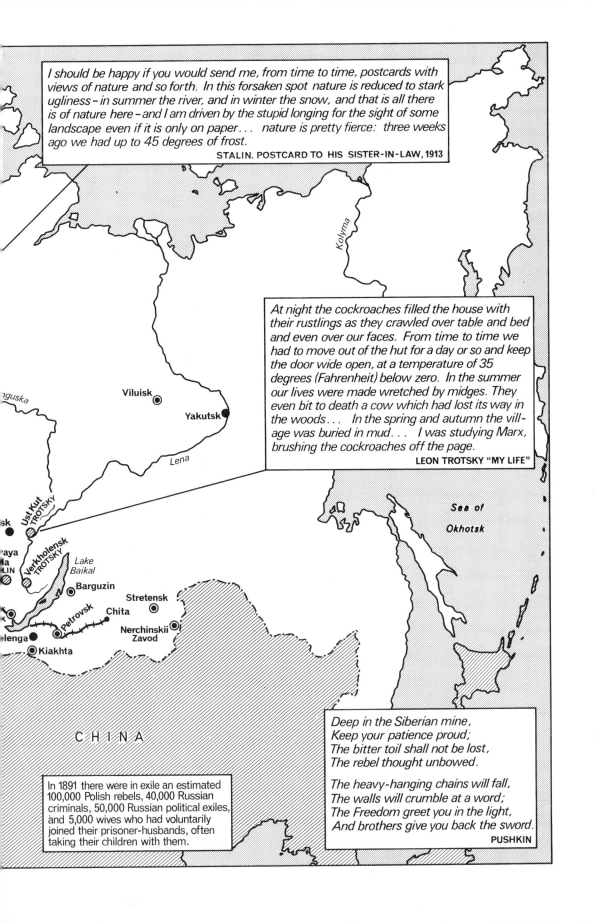

I should be happy if you would send me, from time to time, postcards with views of nature and so forth. In this forsaken spot nature is reduced to stark ugliness – in summer the river, and in winter the snow, and that is all there is of nature here – and I am driven by the stupid longing for the sight of some landscape even if it is only on paper... nature is pretty fierce: three weeks ago we had up to 45 degrees of frost.

STALIN. POSTCARD TO HIS SISTER-IN-LAW, 1913

Kolyma

At night the cockroaches filled the house with their rustlings as they crawled over table and bed and even over our faces. From time to time we had to move out of the hut for a day or so and keep the door wide open, at a temperature of 35 degrees (Fahrenheit) below zero. In the summer our lives were made wretched by midges. They even bit to death a cow which had lost its way in the woods... In the spring and autumn the vill- age was buried in mud... I was studying Marx, brushing the cockroaches off the page.

LEON TROTSKY "MY LIFE"

nguska

Viluisk ◉

Yakutsk ●

Lena

sk

Ust Kut
TROTSKY

Verkholensk
TROTSKY

**aya
la
LIN**

Lake
Baikal

◉ **Barguzin**

Stretensk
◉

Petrovsk **Chita** ◉

Chita

Nerchinskii ◉
Zavod

lenga ●

◉ **Kiakhta**

Sea of
Okhotsk

C H I N A

In 1891 there were in exile an estimated 100,000 Polish rebels, 40,000 Russian criminals, 50,000 Russian political exiles, and 5,000 wives who had voluntarily joined their prisoner-husbands, often taking their children with them.

Deep in the Siberian mine,
Keep your patience proud;
The bitter toil shall not be lost,
The rebel thought unbowed.

The heavy-hanging chains will fall,
The walls will crumble at a word;
The Freedom greet you in the light,
And brothers give you back the sword.

PUSHKIN

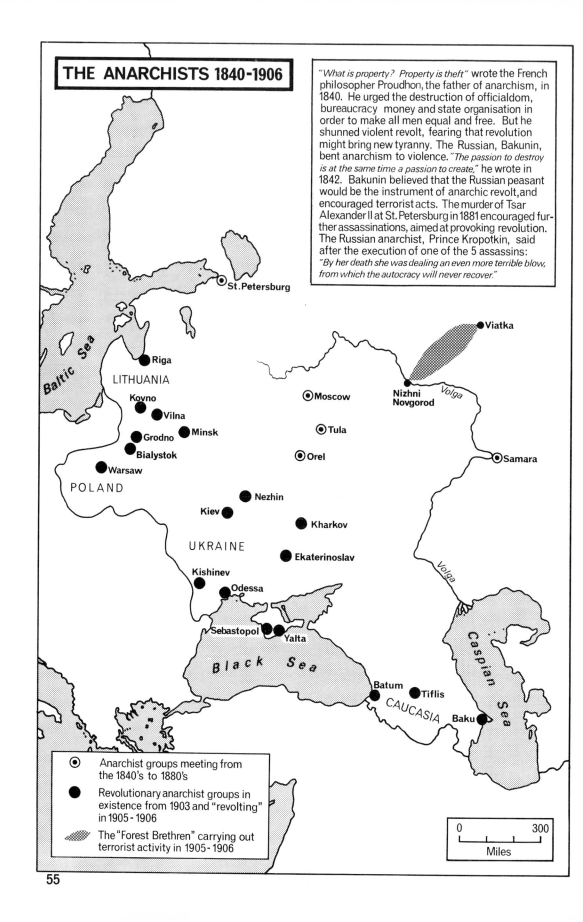

THE ANARCHISTS 1840-1906

"What is property? Property is theft" wrote the French philosopher Proudhon, the father of anarchism, in 1840. He urged the destruction of officialdom, bureaucracy money and state organisation in order to make all men equal and free. But he shunned violent revolt, fearing that revolution might bring new tyranny. The Russian, Bakunin, bent anarchism to violence. "The passion to destroy is at the same time a passion to create," he wrote in 1842. Bakunin believed that the Russian peasant would be the instrument of anarchic revolt, and encouraged terrorist acts. The murder of Tsar Alexander II at St. Petersburg in 1881 encouraged further assassinations, aimed at provoking revolution. The Russian anarchist, Prince Kropotkin, said after the execution of one of the 5 assassins: "By her death she was dealing an even more terrible blow, from which the autocracy will never recover."

St. Petersburg

Viatka

Baltic Sea

Riga

LITHUANIA

Kovno

Vilna

Grodno

Minsk

Bialystok

Warsaw

POLAND

Moscow

Nizhni Novgorod

Volga

Tula

Orel

Samara

Nezhin

Kiev

Kharkov

UKRAINE

Ekaterinoslav

Kishinev

Odessa

Volga

Sebastopol

Yalta

Black Sea

Caspian Sea

Batum

Tiflis

CAUCASIA

Baku

⊙ Anarchist groups meeting from the 1840's to 1880's

● Revolutionary anarchist groups in existence from 1903 and "revolting" in 1905 - 1906

▨ The "Forest Brethren" carrying out terrorist activity in 1905 - 1906

0   300
Miles

55

RUSSIAN INDUSTRY BY 1860

0 — 200
Miles

Archangel

Urals

Vyborg

Viatka

Schlüsselburg

Reval
Narva
St. Petersburg   540,000

Perm   GOLD
Kama   COAL

LEATHER

Yaroslavl

COAL   COPPER

WOOL
Dorpat
Pskov

LINEN

Volga

LEATHER   COPPER

Ufa

Libau
Mitau
Riga
77,000

LEATHER

Tver
Vladimir
Yegorevsk

Moscow   460,000

Nizhni
Novgorod

Kazan
63,000

Baltic Sea

WOOL
Dvinsk

Kovno

Vilna
69,000

Grodno
Bialystok

LINEN

Warsaw
Lodz
LINEN

Dnieper

LINEN

Chernigov

LINEN

Kiev
68,000

Kishinev
94,000

64,000
Nikolaev

Odessa

120,000

Kaluga   Tula
LEATHER

Orel

LINEN

Riazan

LINEN

WOOL
Voronezh

Saratov
84,000

Kharkov

Poltava

Donets

COAL

Don

Volga

Caspian Sea

TOBACCO

Black   Sea

Caucasus

Baku
OIL

POPULATION
1811: **41,000,000**
1863: **74,000,000**

——— The Russian frontier 1815-1914

● Principal cities, with their estimated
  population in 1860

╫╫╫ Railways built by 1860

╊╊╊ Railways under construction in 1860

⊙ Factory development before 1860

◕ Towns with large factory growth
  from 1860

■ Industries expanding rapidly from 1860

▒ Centres of the iron and steel production

▨ Sugar factories

PRINCIPAL IMPORTS: Cotton, machine tools, alcohol,
dyes, fruit and nuts, wool, tea, olive and vegetable oil, silk,
sugar, zinc, steel, iron, copper, horses, cattle, poultry,
salt. Over 80% of all imports and exports went through
the ports of St. Petersburg and Odessa

PRINCIPAL EXPORTS: Wheat, rye, cereals, flour, flax, hemp,
wool, animal fat, lard, seeds, wood, wood products, paper

56

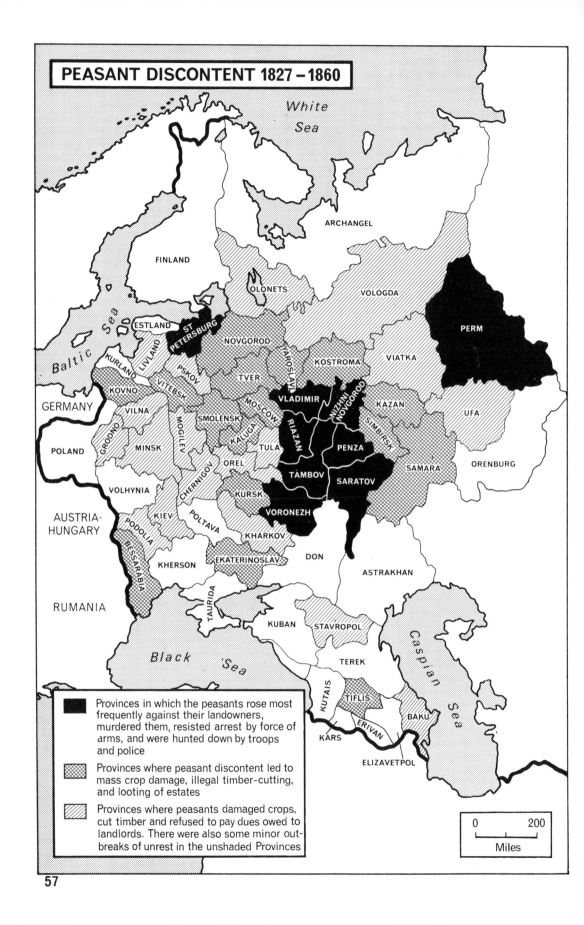

PEASANT DISCONTENT 1827–1860

White Sea

ARCHANGEL

FINLAND

Baltic Sea

OLONETS

VOLOGDA

PERM

ESTLAND
ST PETERSBURG

NOVGOROD

KOSTROMA

VIATKA

KURLAND LIVLAND

PSKOV

YAROSLAVL

GERMANY

KOVNO

VITEBSK

TVER

VLADIMIR

NIZHNI NOVGOROD

KAZAN

UFA

VILNA

MOGILEV

SMOLENSK

MOSCOW

RIAZAN

SIMBIRSK

POLAND

GRODNO

MINSK

KALUGA

TULA

PENZA

ORENBURG

VOLHYNIA

CHERNIGOV

OREL

TAMBOV

SARATOV

SAMARA

AUSTRIA-HUNGARY

PODOLIA

KIEV

POLTAVA

KURSK

VORONEZH

BESSARABIA

KHARKOV

DON

ASTRAKHAN

RUMANIA

KHERSON

EKATERINOSLAV

TAURIDA

Black Sea

KUBAN

STAVROPOL

Caspian Sea

TEREK

KUTAIS

TIFLIS

BAKU

ERIVAN

KARS

ELIZAVETPOL

Provinces in which the peasants rose most frequently against their landowners, murdered them, resisted arrest by force of arms, and were hunted down by troops and police

Provinces where peasant discontent led to mass crop damage, illegal timber-cutting, and looting of estates

Provinces where peasants damaged crops, cut timber and refused to pay dues owed to landlords. There were also some minor outbreaks of unrest in the unshaded Provinces

0   200
Miles

57

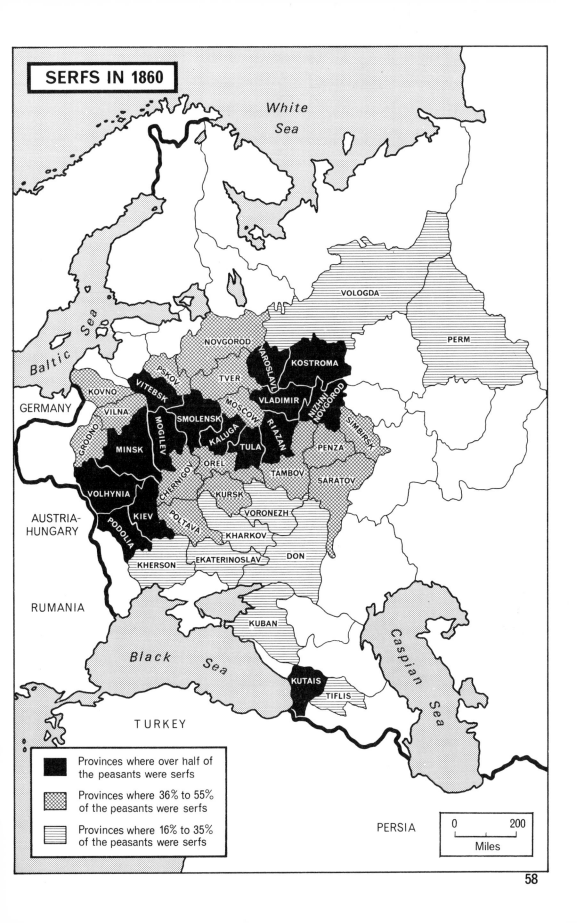

SERFS IN 1860

White Sea

VOLOGDA

PERM

NOVGOROD

Baltic Sea

PSKOV

TVER

YAROSLAVL

KOSTROMA

KOVNO

VITEBSK

VLADIMIR

NIZHNI NOVGOROD

GERMANY

VILNA

MOSCOW

GRODNO

MOGILEV

SMOLENSK

KALUGA

RIAZAN

SIMBIRSK

MINSK

TULA

PENZA

OREL

VOLHYNIA

CHERNIGOV

TAMBOV

SARATOV

KIEV

KURSK

POLTAVA

AUSTRIA-HUNGARY

PODOLIA

VORONEZH

KHARKOV

DON

EKATERINOSLAV

KHERSON

RUMANIA

KUBAN

Black Sea

Caspian Sea

KUTAIS

TIFLIS

TURKEY

Provinces where over half of the peasants were serfs

Provinces where 36% to 55% of the peasants were serfs

Provinces where 16% to 35% of the peasants were serfs

PERSIA

0   200

Miles

58

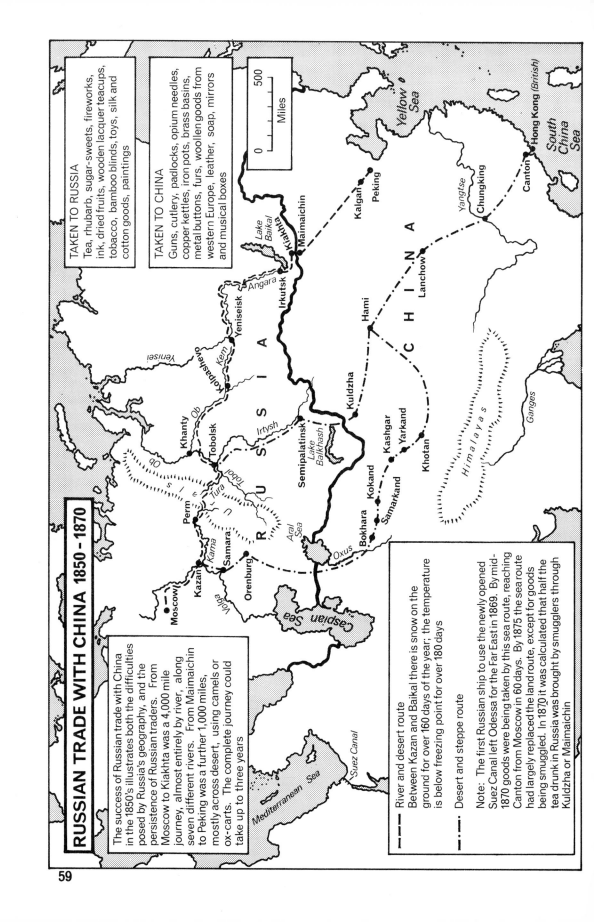

RUSSIAN TRADE WITH CHINA 1850 – 1870

The success of Russian trade with China in the 1850's illustrates both the difficulties posed by Russia's geography, and the persistence of Russian traders. From Moscow to Kiakhta was a 4,000 mile journey, almost entirely by river, along seven different rivers. From Maimaichin to Peking was a further 1,000 miles, mostly across desert, using camels or ox-carts. The complete journey could take up to three years

TAKEN TO RUSSIA
Tea, rhubarb, sugar-sweets, fireworks, ink, dried fruits, wooden lacquer teacups, tobacco, bamboo blinds, toys, silk and cotton goods, paintings

TAKEN TO CHINA
Guns, cutlery, padlocks, opium needles, copper kettles, iron pots, brass basins, metal buttons, furs, woollen goods from western Europe, leather, soap, mirrors and musical boxes

- - - River and desert route
Between Kazan and Baikal there is snow on the ground for over 160 days of the year; the temperature is below freezing point for over 180 days

-·- Desert and steppe route

Note: The first Russian ship to use the newly opened Suez Canal left Odessa for the Far East in 1869. By mid-1870 goods were being taken by this sea route, reaching Canton from Moscow in 60 days. By 1875 the sea route had largely replaced the land route, except for goods being smuggled. In 1870 it was calculated that half the tea drunk in Russia was brought by smugglers through Kuldzha or Maimaichin

500
0   Miles

59

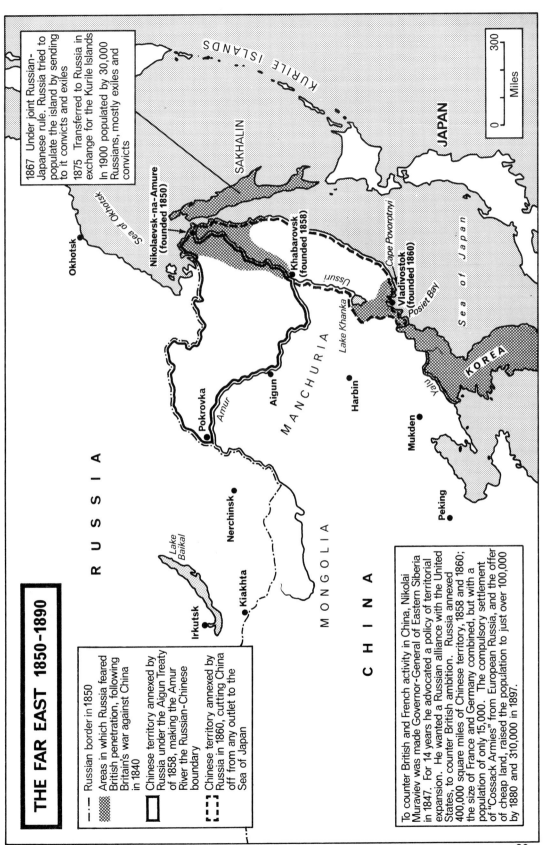

THE FAR EAST 1850-1890

1867 Under joint Russian-Japanese rule. Russia tried to populate the island by sending to it convicts and exiles

1875 Transferred to Russia in exchange for the Kurile Islands In 1900 populated by 30,000 Russians, mostly exiles and convicts

KURILE ISLANDS

SAKHALIN

JAPAN

Sea of Okhotsk

Nikolaevsk-na-Amure (founded 1850)

Khabarovsk (founded 1858)

Cape Povorotnyi

Vladivostok (founded 1860)

Posiet Bay

Sea of Japan

Ussuri

Okhotsk

Lake Khanka

KOREA

MANCHURIA

Harbin

Yalu

Pokrovka

Amur

Aigun

Mukden

R U S S I A

Lake Baikal

Nerchinsk

MONGOLIA

Peking

Irkutsk

Kiakhta

C H I N A

Legend

- – – Russian border in 1850

Areas in which Russia feared British penetration, following Britain's war against China in 1840

Chinese territory annexed by Russia under the Aigun Treaty of 1858, making the Amur River the Russian-Chinese boundary

Chinese territory annexed by Russia in 1860, cutting China off from any outlet to the Sea of Japan

To counter British and French activity in China, Nikolai Muraviev was made Governor-General of Eastern Siberia in 1847. For 14 years he advocated a policy of territorial expansion. He wanted a Russian alliance with the United States, to counter British ambition. Russia annexed 400,000 square miles of Chinese territory, 1858 and 1860; the size of France and Germany combined, but with a population of only 15,000. The compulsory settlement of "Cossack Armies" from European Russia, and the offer of cheap land, raised the population to just over 100,000 by 1880 and 310,000 in 1897.

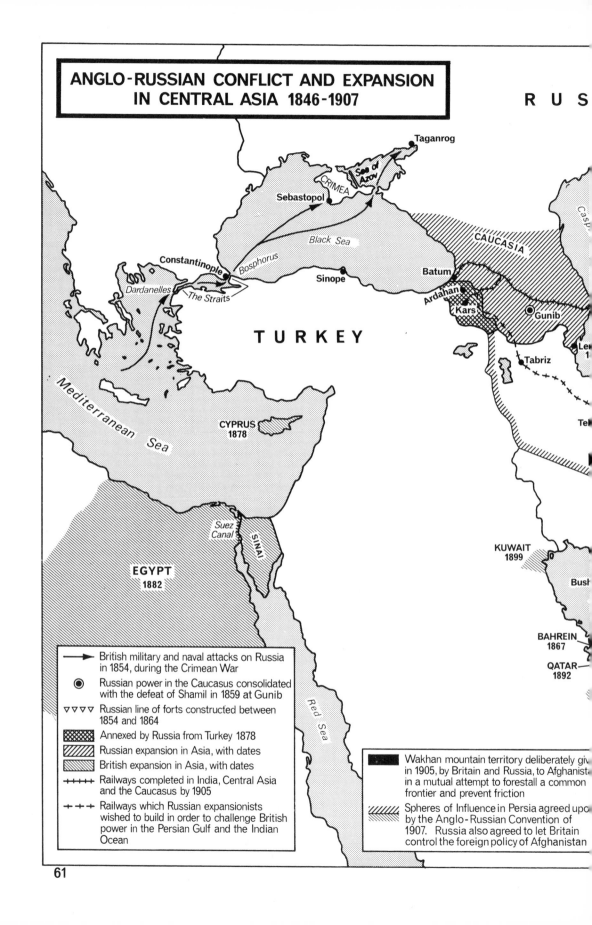

ANGLO-RUSSIAN CONFLICT AND EXPANSION IN CENTRAL ASIA 1846-1907

R U S

Taganrog

Sea of Azov

CRIMEA

Sebastopol

Black Sea

Casp

CAUCASIA

Constantinople

Bosphorus

Batum

Dardanelles

The Straits

Sinope

Ardahan

Kars

Gunib

Le

TURKEY

Tabriz

Mediterranean

Sea

CYPRUS
1878

Te

Suez
Canal

SINAI

KUWAIT
1899

EGYPT
1882

Bus

BAHREIN
1867

Red Sea

QATAR
1892

→ British military and naval attacks on Russia in 1854, during the Crimean War

◉ Russian power in the Caucasus consolidated with the defeat of Shamil in 1859 at Gunib

▽▽▽ Russian line of forts constructed between 1854 and 1864

▨ Annexed by Russia from Turkey 1878

▨ Russian expansion in Asia, with dates

▨ British expansion in Asia, with dates

+++++ Railways completed in India, Central Asia and the Caucasus by 1905

+ + + Railways which Russian expansionists wished to build in order to challenge British power in the Persian Gulf and the Indian Ocean

▨ Wakhan mountain territory deliberately giv in 1905, by Britain and Russia, to Afghanist in a mutual attempt to forestall a common frontier and prevent friction

▨ Spheres of Influence in Persia agreed upo by the Anglo-Russian Convention of 1907. Russia also agreed to let Britain control the foreign policy of Afghanistan

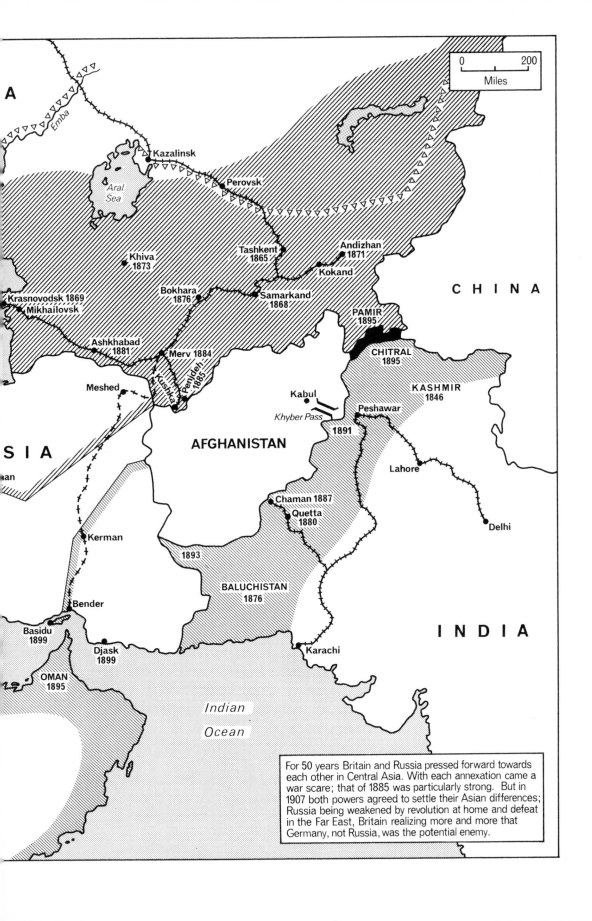

A

Emba

Kazalinsk

Aral Sea

Perovsk

Tashkent
1865

Andizhan
1871

Kokand

CHINA

Khiva
1873

Krasnovodsk 1869
Mikhailovsk

Bokhara
1876

Samarkand
1868

PAMIR
1895

Ashkhabad
1881

Merv 1884

CHITRAL
1895

Meshed

Penjdeh
1885

Kushka

KASHMIR
1846

Kabul

Peshawar

Khyber Pass
1891

SIA

AFGHANISTAN

Lahore

an

Kerman

Chaman 1887
Quetta
1880

Delhi

1893

Bender

BALUCHISTAN
1876

INDIA

Basidu
1899

Djask
1899

Karachi

OMAN
1895

Indian

Ocean

0 _____ 200
Miles

For 50 years Britain and Russia pressed forward towards
each other in Central Asia. With each annexation came a
war scare; that of 1885 was particularly strong. But in
1907 both powers agreed to settle their Asian differences;
Russia being weakened by revolution at home and defeat
in the Far East, Britain realizing more and more that
Germany, not Russia, was the potential enemy.

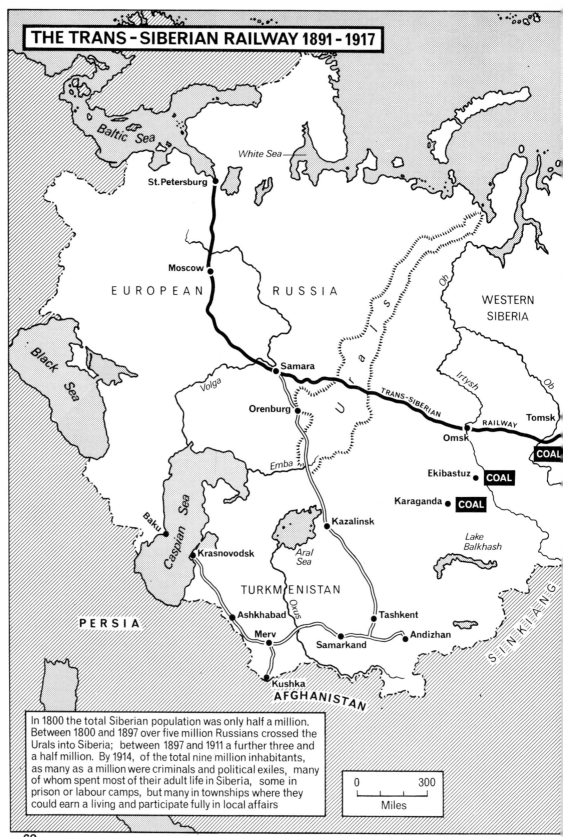

THE TRANS-SIBERIAN RAILWAY 1891-1917

Baltic Sea

White Sea

St. Petersburg

Moscow

EUROPEAN   RUSSIA

WESTERN
SIBERIA

Black
Sea

Samara

Volga

Orenburg

Ob

U r a l s

Irtysh

TRANS-SIBERIAN

Omsk   RAILWAY   Tomsk

Ob

Emba

COAL

Ekibastuz **COAL**

Karaganda **COAL**

Baku

Caspian Sea

Kazalinsk

Aral
Sea

Lake
Balkhash

Krasnovodsk

TURKMENISTAN

Oxus

PERSIA

Ashkhabad

Merv

Samarkand

Tashkent

Andizhan

S I N K I A N G

Kushka
AFGHANISTAN

In 1800 the total Siberian population was only half a million.
Between 1800 and 1897 over five million Russians crossed the
Urals into Siberia; between 1897 and 1911 a further three and
a half million. By 1914, of the total nine million inhabitants,
as many as a million were criminals and political exiles, many
of whom spent most of their adult life in Siberia, some in
prison or labour camps, but many in townships where they
could earn a living and participate fully in local affairs

0   300

Miles

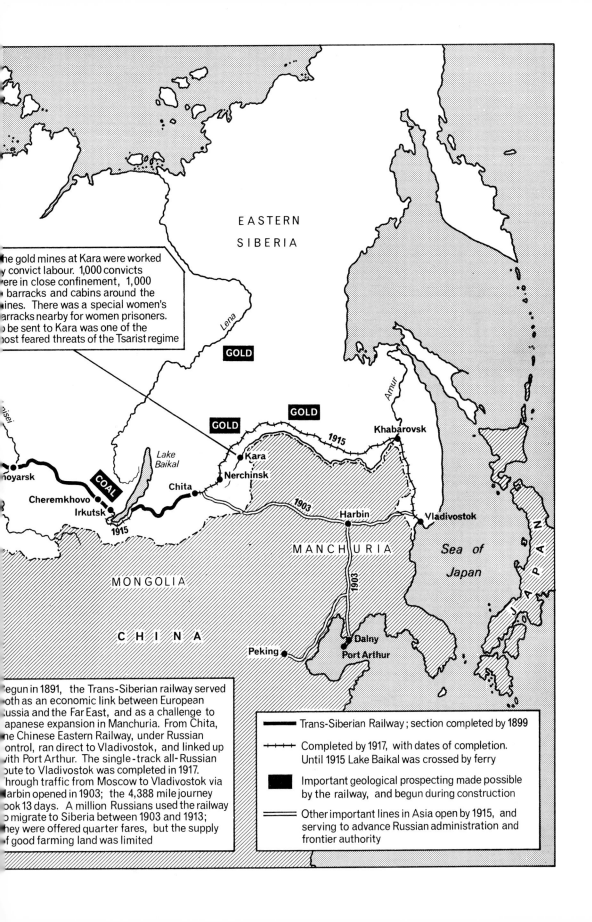

EASTERN
SIBERIA

The gold mines at Kara were worked
by convict labour. 1,000 convicts
were in close confinement, 1,000
in barracks and cabins around the
mines. There was a special women's
barracks nearby for women prisoners.
To be sent to Kara was one of the
most feared threats of the Tsarist regime

Lena

Amur

GOLD

GOLD

GOLD

Khabarovsk

1915

Kara

*Lake
Baikal*

Nerchinsk

noyarsk

COAL

Chita

1903

Cheremkhovo

Harbin

Vladivostok

Irkutsk

1915

MANCHURIA

*Sea of
Japan*

MONGOLIA

1903

J
A
P
A
N

CHINA

Dalny

Peking

Port Arthur

Begun in 1891, the Trans-Siberian railway served
both as an economic link between European
Russia and the Far East, and as a challenge to
Japanese expansion in Manchuria. From Chita,
the Chinese Eastern Railway, under Russian
control, ran direct to Vladivostok, and linked up
with Port Arthur. The single-track all-Russian
route to Vladivostok was completed in 1917.
Through traffic from Moscow to Vladivostok via
Harbin opened in 1903; the 4,388 mile journey
took 13 days. A million Russians used the railway
to migrate to Siberia between 1903 and 1913;
they were offered quarter fares, but the supply
of good farming land was limited

———— Trans-Siberian Railway; section completed by 1899

+++++ Completed by 1917, with dates of completion.
Until 1915 Lake Baikal was crossed by ferry

████ Important geological prospecting made possible
by the railway, and begun during construction

═══ Other important lines in Asia open by 1915, and
serving to advance Russian administration and
frontier authority

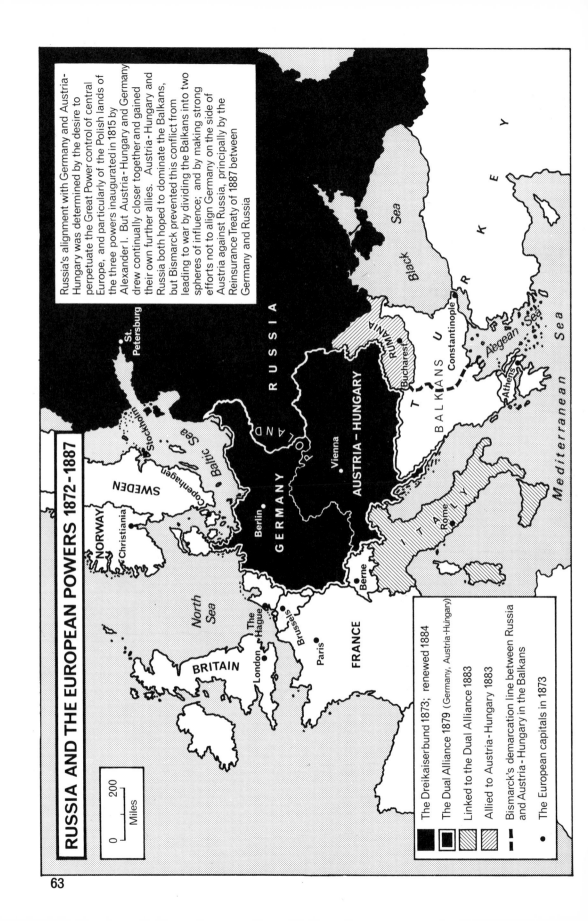

RUSSIA AND THE EUROPEAN POWERS 1872-1887

Russia's alignment with Germany and Austria-Hungary was determined by the desire to perpetuate the Great Power control of central Europe, and particularly of the Polish lands of the three powers inaugurated in 1815 by Alexander I. But Austria-Hungary and Germany drew continually closer together and gained their own further allies. Austria-Hungary and Russia both hoped to dominate the Balkans, but Bismarck prevented this conflict from leading to war by dividing the Balkans into two spheres of influence; and by making strong efforts not to align Germany on the side of Austria against Russia, principally by the Reinsurance Treaty of 1887 between Germany and Russia

The Dreikaiserbund 1873; renewed 1884

The Dual Alliance 1879 (Germany, Austria-Hungary)

Linked to the Dual Alliance 1883

Allied to Austria-Hungary 1883

Bismarck's demarcation line between Russia and Austria-Hungary in the Balkans

The European capitals in 1873

NORWAY
SWEDEN
Christiania
Stockholm
Copenhagen
St. Petersburg
RUSSIA
POLAND
GERMANY
Berlin
AUSTRIA–HUNGARY
Vienna
Berne
ITALY
Rome
FRANCE
Paris
Brussels
The Hague
London
BRITAIN
North Sea
Baltic Sea
Black Sea
RUMANIA
Bucharest
TURKEY
Constantinople
BALKANS
Athens
Aegean Sea
Mediterranean Sea

0 200
Miles

63

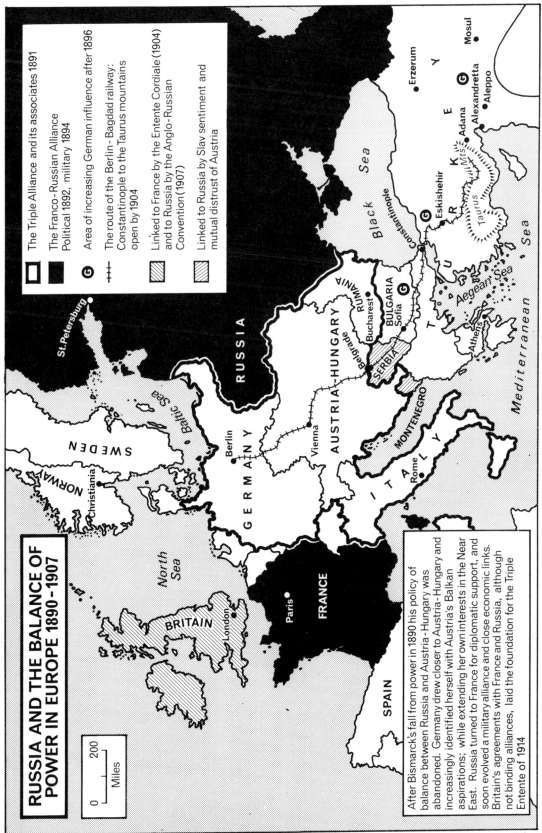

RUSSIA AND THE BALANCE OF POWER IN EUROPE 1890–1907

The Triple Alliance and its associates 1891

The Franco-Russian Alliance Political 1892, military 1894

Area of increasing German influence after 1896

The route of the Berlin - Bagdad railway: Constantinople to the Taurus mountains open by 1904

Linked to France by the Entente Cordiale (1904) and to Russia by the Anglo-Russian Convention (1907)

Linked to Russia by Slav sentiment and mutual distrust of Austria

After Bismarck's fall from power in 1890 his policy of balance between Russia and Austria-Hungary was abandoned. Germany drew closer to Austria-Hungary and increasingly identified herself with Austria's Balkan aspirations; while extending her own interests in the Near East. Russia turned to France for diplomatic support, and soon evolved a military alliance and close economic links. Britain's agreements with France and Russia, although not binding alliances, laid the foundation for the Triple Entente of 1914

0   200
Miles

SWEDEN

NORWAY

Christiania

St.Petersburg

Baltic Sea

North Sea

BRITAIN

London

Paris

FRANCE

SPAIN

GERMANY

Berlin

Vienna

AUSTRIA-HUNGARY

ITALY

Rome

MONTENEGRO

SERBIA

Belgrade

RUMANIA

Bucharest

BULGARIA

Sofia

RUSSIA

Black Sea

Constantinople

Eskishehir

TURKEY

Taurus Mts.

Erzerum

Mosul

Alexandretta

Adana

Aleppo

Athens

Aegean Sea

Mediterranean Sea

64

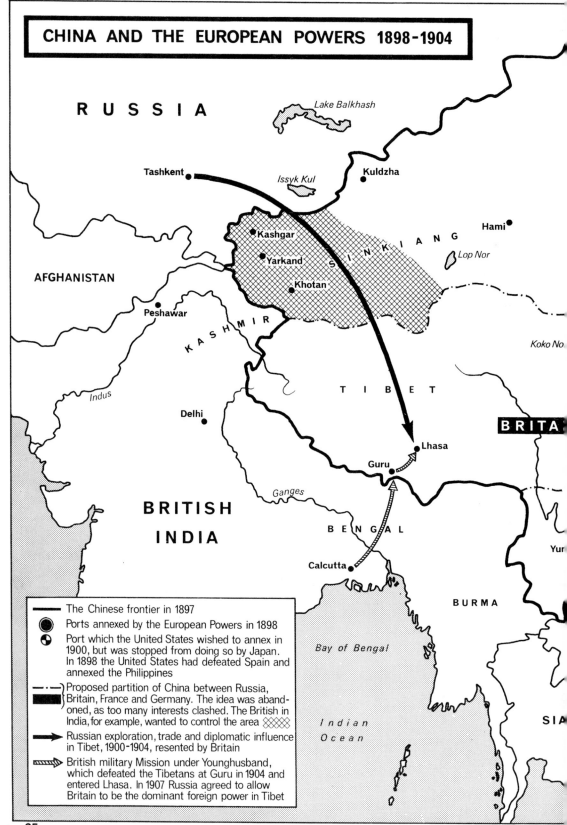

CHINA AND THE EUROPEAN POWERS 1898-1904

RUSSIA

Lake Balkhash

Tashkent

Issyk Kul

Kuldzha

Hami

Kashgar

S I N K I A N G

Lop Nor

Yarkand

Khotan

AFGHANISTAN

Koko No.

Peshawar

K A S H M I R

Indus

T I B E T

Delhi

BRITA

Lhasa

Guru

Ganges

BRITISH

INDIA

B E N G A L

Calcutta

Yur

BURMA

The Chinese frontier in 1897

Ports annexed by the European Powers in 1898

Port which the United States wished to annex in 1900, but was stopped from doing so by Japan. In 1898 the United States had defeated Spain and annexed the Philippines

Proposed partition of China between Russia, Britain, France and Germany. The idea was abandoned, as too many interests clashed. The British in India, for example, wanted to control the area ⬚⬚⬚⬚

Russian exploration, trade and diplomatic influence in Tibet, 1900-1904, resented by Britain

British military Mission under Younghusband, which defeated the Tibetans at Guru in 1904 and entered Lhasa. In 1907 Russia agreed to allow Britain to be the dominant foreign power in Tibet

Bay of Bengal

Indian Ocean

SIA

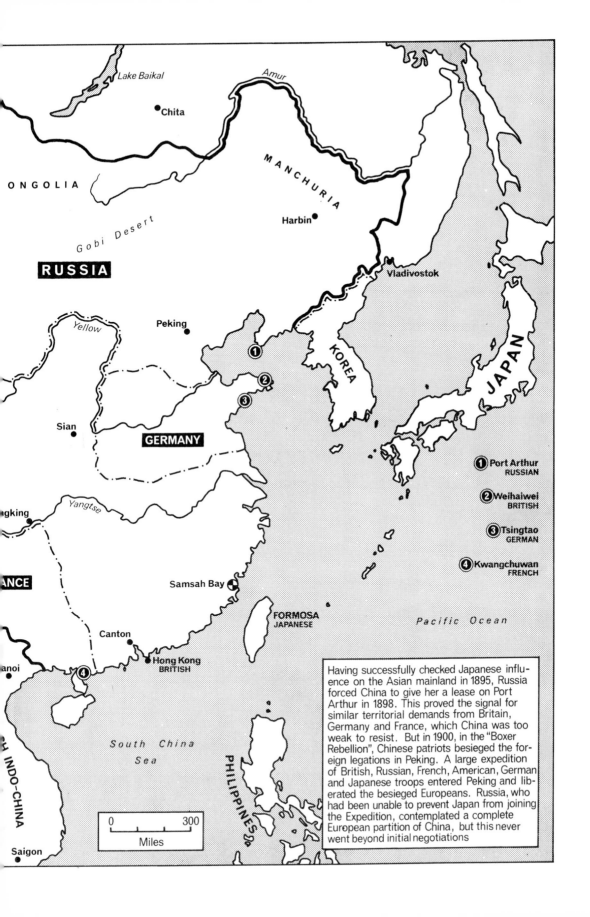

Lake Baikal

Amur

•Chita

MANCHURIA

ONGOLIA

Gobi Desert

Harbin•

RUSSIA

Vladivostok

Yellow

Peking •

①

②

③

KOREA

JAPAN

Sian •

GERMANY

① Port Arthur
RUSSIAN

② Weihaiwei
BRITISH

③ Tsingtao
GERMAN

④ Kwangchuwan
FRENCH

Yangtse

gking •

NCE

Samsah Bay

FORMOSA
JAPANESE

Pacific Ocean

Canton •

anoi

④

Hong Kong
BRITISH

South China
Sea

PHILIPPINES

H INDO-CHINA

Saigon
•

Having successfully checked Japanese influence on the Asian mainland in 1895, Russia
forced China to give her a lease on Port
Arthur in 1898. This proved the signal for
similar territorial demands from Britain,
Germany and France, which China was too
weak to resist. But in 1900, in the "Boxer
Rebellion", Chinese patriots besieged the foreign legations in Peking. A large expedition
of British, Russian, French, American, German
and Japanese troops entered Peking and lib-
erated the besieged Europeans. Russia, who
had been unable to prevent Japan from joining
the Expedition, contemplated a complete
European partition of China, but this never
went beyond initial negotiations

0   300
Miles

RUSSIA AND JAPAN IN THE FAR EAST 1860-1895

Kamchatka: part of Russia in 1650. Since 1750 used largely as a place of exile for criminals and political prisoners. Russian schoolboys were often threatened that slackers would be "sent to Kamchatka"– the furthest corner of the classroom. The peninsula has over 20 active volcanoes.

The struggle between Russia and Japan in the Far East was long and bitter. In 1860 Russia acquired an outlet on the Sea of Japan. The Japanese at once adopted a forward policy in China and Korea. When Japan defeated China in 1895 she expected to make wide territorial gains. But Russia, France, Britain and Germany combined to deprive Japan of the fruits of victory. This led to deep anti-Russian resentment throughout Japan. Throughout this period, European penetration in south China continued unabated.

KAMCHATKA

SIBERIA

Sea of Okhotsk

Petropavlovsk

RUSSIA

Amur

EASTERN

Nikolaevsk

SAKHALIN

KURILE ISLANDS

MANCHURIA

Khabarosvk

Uruppu

Harbin

Sungari

Ussuri

Etorofu

Changchun

Kirin

Mukden

Vladivostok

Peking

Yalu

Sea of Japan

Pacific

Tientsin

Wonsan

Port Arthur

Seoul

Weihaiwei

Inchon

KOREA

Ocean

Tsingtao

Yellow

Yellow Sea

Pusan

JAPAN

0   500
Miles

Nanking

Hankow

Shanghai

Yangtse

Oshima

Okinawa

RYUKYU ISLANDS

Macao (Portuguese 1557)

Kowloon (British 1861)

Hongkong (British 1841)

FORMOSA

South China Sea

PHILIPPINES
(Spanish 1521)

- ■ Territory annexed by Russia from China in 1858-1860
- ⌐ ⌐ Islands annexed by Japan from China in 1874
- ⋮⋮⋮ Islands annexed by Japan in return for Russian control of Sakhalin
- ◉ Korean ports open, as the result of Japanese pressure, to Japanese trade 1876-1878
- ▨ Occupied by Japan during the war with China, 1894-95. Russia, France, Britain and Germany combined to prevent Japan keeping any of this territory
- ▭ Only Chinese territory actually annexed by Japan after the war of 1894-1895

66

0   300
Miles

WAR DEAD 1904-05
Russian   120,000
Japanese   75,000

RUSSIA

Chita
Nerchinsk
Amur
Nikolaevsk
Argun
SAKHALIN
Hailar
MANCHURIA
Khabarovsk
Tsitsihar
Amur
Harbin
Sungari
CHINA
Mukden
Vladivostok
Yalu
Peking
Sea of Japan
Port
Arthur
KOREA
Seoul
Yellow
Sea
Tokyo
Tsushima Strait
JAPAN

The Trans-Siberian Railway by 1895

Under increasing Russian control after 1895

Leased by Russia from China in 1898, together with the right to build a railway to Harbin; (completed by 1904)

The Chinese Eastern Railway, controlled by Russia after its completion in 1903

Russian economic penetration. Russia refused to allow Japan a sphere of influence in Korea

Japanese naval and military attacks 1904-1905

Annexed by Japan in 1905

After successfully halting Japanese expansion in 1895, the Russians adopted an active expansionist policy. For 10 years they pressed forward in Manchuria, and discussed the partition of China with the British Government in 1900. But Japan sought revenge for the humiliation of 1895, and in 1902 neutralized Britain by the Anglo-Japanese Alliance. In February 1904, under Russian provocation, Japan attacked Port Arthur. Russia was defeated on land and sea, and a peace treaty was signed in the United States in Sept. 1905. The grave demoralization created by Russia's defeat led to a mass of revolutionary outbreaks in Russia, and to a serious weakening of the Tsarist mystique.

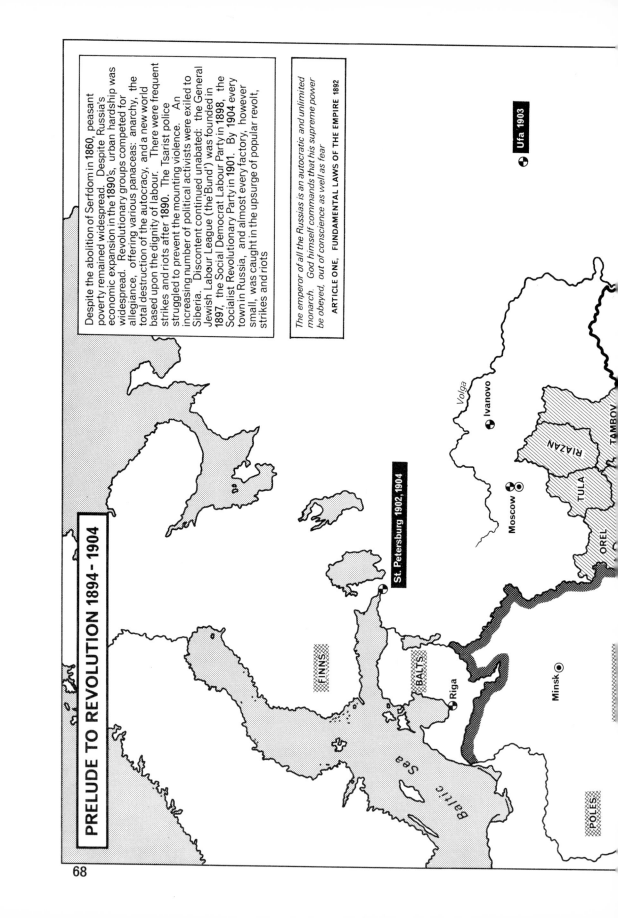

PRELUDE TO REVOLUTION 1894 - 1904

Despite the abolition of Serfdom in 1860, peasant poverty remained widespread. Despite Russia's economic expansion in the 1890's, urban hardship was widespread. Revolutionary groups competed for allegiance, offering various panaceas: anarchy, the total destruction of the autocracy, and a new world based upon the dignity of labour. There were frequent strikes and riots after 1890. The Tsarist police struggled to prevent the mounting violence. An increasing number of political activists were exiled to Siberia. Discontent continued unabated: the General Jewish Labour League (the 'Bund') was founded in 1897, the Social Democrat Labour Party in 1898, the Socialist Revolutionary Party in 1901. By 1904 every town in Russia, and almost every factory, however small, was caught in the upsurge of popular revolt, strikes and riots

The emperor of all the Russias is an autocratic and unlimited monarch. God himself commands that his supreme power be obeyed, out of conscience as well as fear

ARTICLE ONE, FUNDAMENTAL LAWS OF THE EMPIRE 1892

Ufa 1903

Volga

Ivanovo

RIAZAN

TULA

TAMBOV

OREL

Moscow

St. Petersburg 1902, 1904

FINNS

BALTS

Riga

Minsk

Baltic Sea

POLES

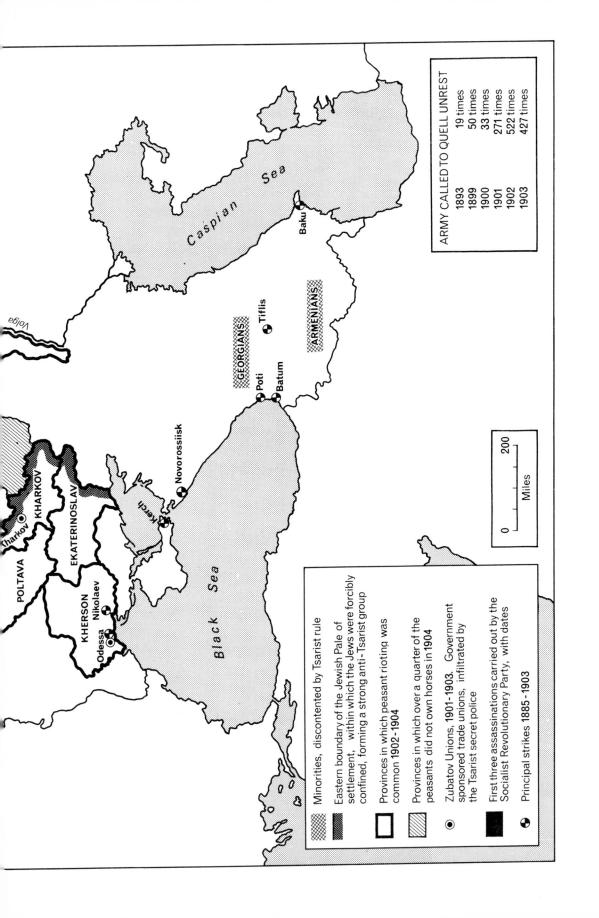

ARMY CALLED TO QUELL UNREST

1893	19 times
1899	50 times
1900	33 times
1901	271 times
1902	522 times
1903	427 times

Caspian Sea

Volga

Baku

GEORGIANS

Tiflis

ARMENIANS

Poti

Batum

Novorossiisk

Kerch

Black Sea

POLTAVA

KHARKOV

Kharkov

EKATERINOSLAV

KHERSON

Nikolaev

Odessa

0   200
Miles

Minorities, discontented by Tsarist rule

Eastern boundary of the Jewish Pale of settlement, within which the Jews were forcibly confined, forming a strong anti-Tsarist group

Provinces in which peasant rioting was common 1902-1904

Provinces in which over a quarter of the peasants did not own horses in 1904

Zubatov Unions, 1901-1903. Government sponsored trade unions, infiltrated by the Tsarist secret police

First three assassinations carried out by the Socialist Revolutionary Party, with dates

Principal strikes 1885-1903

THE JEWS AND THEIR ENEMIES 1648-1917

1903 / 1906 St.Petersburg

Tsarskoye Selo △ 1905

1891. 2,000 Jews depor
many of them in chains

Baltic Sea

⊙ Dusiata

Mogilev ⊙

Minsk ⊙

Starodub ⊙

⊙ Bialystok

Gomel ⊙

Berlin △ 1911

Sedlits ⊙

Brest-Litovsk ⊙

Konotop ⊙

Nezhin ⊙

⊙ Xanten

GERMANY

Lodz ⊙

Czestochowa ⊙

Kiev ⊙

Zhitomir ⊙

Pereyaslavl ⊙

Sm ⊙

Elizavetgrad ⊙

Balta ⊙

Tisza-Eszlar ✛

Anana ⊙

Nikolaevk

AUSTRIA - HUNGARY

Kishinev ⊙

Odessa ⊙

RUMANIA

BULGARIA ✛

///// Area in which the Ukrainian peasantry,
led by Bogdan Khmelnitski, massacred
over 100,000 Jews 1648-1656

☐ The Pale of Settlement inside Russia, to
which Russian Jews were confined by law
1815-1917. Of Russia's 5 million Jews
in 1880, only 300,000 had managed to
live outside, mostly illegally

⊙ Principal mob attacks, or "pogroms",
against Jews, 1871-1906

✛ Ritual murder charges, in Russia and
elsewhere, in which Jews were accused
of using the blood of Christian children
to mix with their Passover bread. These
charges led to harsh mob violence
against the Jews

△ Publishing centres before 1917 of the anti-
semitic forgery, "Protocols of Zion", which
claimed to be the Jewish plan for world
domination

Vologda

The three main anti-Jewish groups in Imperial Russia were the peasants and Cossacks of the Ukraine, the intellectual Slavophils, and the Tsarist Government, and aristocracy. The peasants and Cossacks saw the rich Jew as an exploiter, the poor Jew as a rival, and the intellectual Jew as a dangerous revolutionary. The Slavophils believed in the sacred mission of the Slav peoples, under the guidance of their Orthodox Tsar; they wanted Russia to adopt a strong pro-Slav, and anti-Turk policy, and saw the Jew as anti-Christ, an alien on Russian soil, and a subversive influence acting against Russian interests. Both peasants and Slavophils were in many ways supported by the Government, whose laws discriminated against the Jews, and whose Pale of Settlement confined them

Nizhni
Novgorod ◉

◉ Murom   ◉ Simbirsk

Moscow

91. 20,000 Jews expelled

● Saratov

◉ Tsaritsyn

erinoslav   ◉ Rostov

itopol
◉

● Simferopol

ack   Sea   ● Kutais

Caspian Sea

200
Miles

National boundaries
of 1914

1882 500,000 Jews living in rural areas
of the Pale were forced to leave their homes
and live in towns or townlets (shtetls) in the
Pale. 250,000 Jews living along the western
frontier zone were also moved into the
Pale. A further 700,000 Jews living east of
the Pale were driven into the Pale by 1891

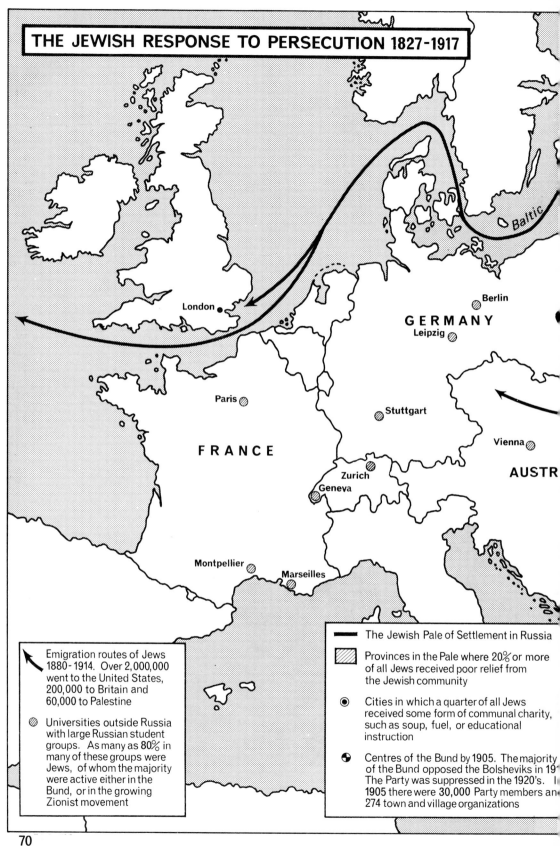

THE JEWISH RESPONSE TO PERSECUTION 1827-1917

Baltic

Berlin

GERMANY

Leipzig

London

Paris

Stuttgart

Vienna

FRANCE

Zurich
Geneva

AUSTR

Montpellier

Marseilles

—— The Jewish Pale of Settlement in Russia

Provinces in the Pale where 20% or more
of all Jews received poor relief from
the Jewish community

◉ Cities in which a quarter of all Jews
received some form of communal charity,
such as soup, fuel, or educational
instruction

Centres of the Bund by 1905. The majority
of the Bund opposed the Bolsheviks in 19
The Party was suppressed in the 1920's. I
1905 there were **30,000** Party members an
274 town and village organizations

Emigration routes of Jews
1880-1914. Over 2,000,000
went to the United States,
200,000 to Britain and
60,000 to Palestine

Universities outside Russia
with large Russian student
groups. As many as 80% in
many of these groups were
Jews, of whom the majority
were active either in the
Bund, or in the growing
Zionist movement

70

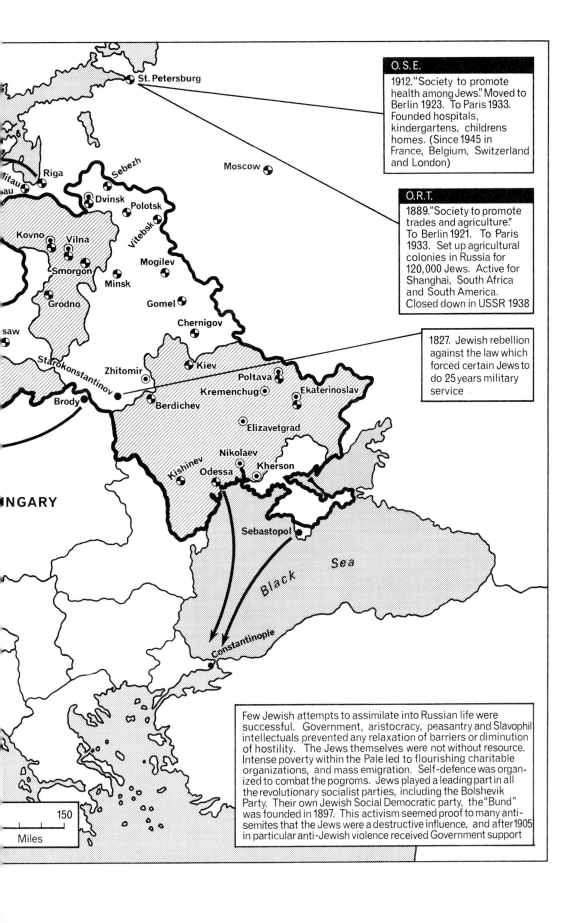

St. Petersburg

O.S.E.

1912. "Society to promote health among Jews." Moved to Berlin 1923. To Paris 1933. Founded hospitals, kindergartens, childrens homes. (Since 1945 in France, Belgium, Switzerland and London)

O.R.T.

1889. "Society to promote trades and agriculture." To Berlin 1921. To Paris 1933. Set up agricultural colonies in Russia for 120,000 Jews. Active for Shanghai, South Africa and South America. Closed down in USSR 1938

Riga

Mitau
au

Sebezh

Moscow

Dvinsk

Polotsk

Vitebsk

Kovno

Vilna

Mogilev

Smorgon

Minsk

Grodno

Gomel

Chernigov

1827. Jewish rebellion against the law which forced certain Jews to do 25 years military service

saw

Starokonstantinov

Zhitomir

Kiev

Poltava

Kremenchug

Ekaterinoslav

Brody

Berdichev

Elizavetgrad

Nikolaev

Kishinev

Odessa

Kherson

NGARY

Sebastopol

Black   Sea

Constantinople

Few Jewish attempts to assimilate into Russian life were successful. Government, aristocracy, peasantry and Slavophil intellectuals prevented any relaxation of barriers or diminution of hostility. The Jews themselves were not without resource. Intense poverty within the Pale led to flourishing charitable organizations, and mass emigration. Self-defence was organized to combat the pogroms. Jews played a leading part in all the revolutionary socialist parties, including the Bolshevik Party. Their own Jewish Social Democratic party, the "Bund" was founded in 1897. This activism seemed proof to many anti-semites that the Jews were a destructive influence, and after 1905 in particular anti-Jewish violence received Government support

150

Miles

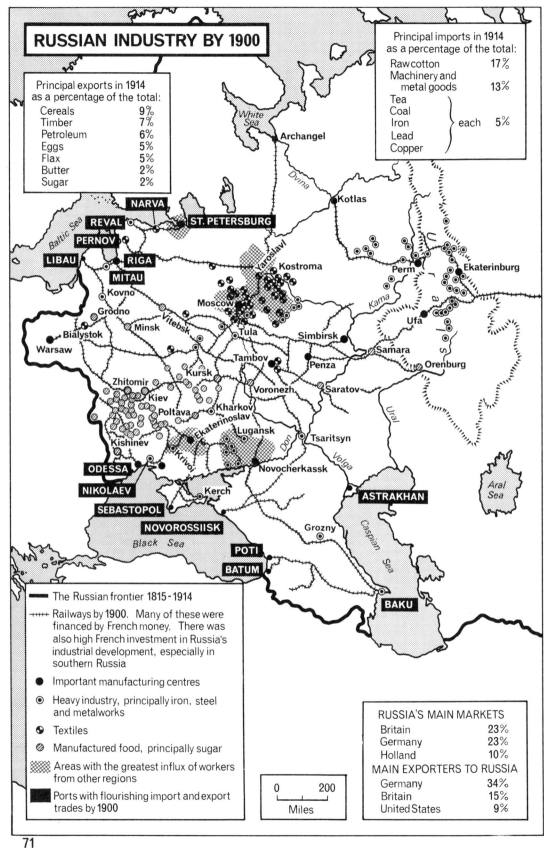

RUSSIAN INDUSTRY BY 1900

Principal exports in 1914
as a percentage of the total:

Cereals	9%
Timber	7%
Petroleum	6%
Eggs	5%
Flax	5%
Butter	2%
Sugar	2%

Principal imports in 1914
as a percentage of the total:

Raw cotton	17%
Machinery and metal goods	13%
Tea	
Coal	
Iron	each 5%
Lead	
Copper	

White Sea
Archangel
Dvina
Kotlas
NARVA
REVAL
PERNOV
ST. PETERSBURG
Baltic Sea
LIBAU
RIGA
MITAU
Kovno
Grodno
Minsk
Vitebsk
Moscow
Tula
Bialystok
Warsaw
Zhitomir
Kiev
Poltava
Kursk
Tambov
Voronezh
Kharkov
Ekaterinoslav
Lugansk
Kishinev
Krivoi
ODESSA
NIKOLAEV
SEBASTOPOL
Kerch
NOVOROSSIISK
Black Sea
POTI
BATUM
Yaroslavl
Kostroma
Simbirsk
Penza
Saratov
Don
Tsaritsyn
Novocherkassk
Grozny
Volga
ASTRAKHAN
Caspian Sea
BAKU
Perm
Ekaterinburg
Kama
Ufa
Samara
Orenburg
Ural
Aral Sea
Minsk

The Russian frontier 1815-1914

+++++ Railways by 1900. Many of these were
financed by French money. There was
also high French investment in Russia's
industrial development, especially in
southern Russia

● Important manufacturing centres

◉ Heavy industry, principally iron, steel
and metalworks

◕ Textiles

⊘ Manufactured food, principally sugar

▦ Areas with the greatest influx of workers
from other regions

▮ Ports with flourishing import and export
trades by 1900

0   200
Miles

RUSSIA'S MAIN MARKETS	
Britain	23%
Germany	23%
Holland	10%
MAIN EXPORTERS TO RUSSIA	
Germany	34%
Britain	15%
United States	9%

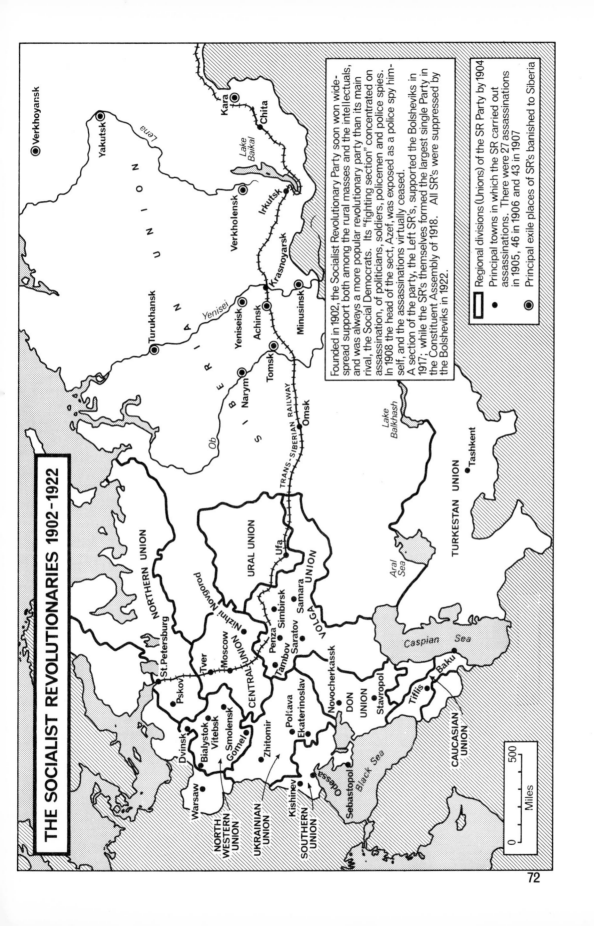

THE SOCIALIST REVOLUTIONARIES 1902-1922

Founded in 1902, the Socialist Revolutionary Party soon won wide-spread support both among the rural masses and the intellectuals, and was always a more popular revolutionary party than its main rival, the Social Democrats. Its "fighting section" concentrated on assassination, of politicians, soldiers, policemen and police spies. In 1908 the head of the sect, Azef, was exposed as a police spy himself, and the assassinations virtually ceased.

A section of the party, the Left SR's, supported the Bolsheviks in 1917; while the SR's themselves formed the largest single Party in the Constituent Assembly of 1918. All SR's were suppressed by the Bolsheviks in 1922.

☐ Regional divisions (Unions) of the SR Party by 1904

• Principal towns in which the SR carried out assassinations. There were 27 assassinations in 1905, 46 in 1906 and 43 in 1907

◉ Principal exile places of SR's banished to Siberia

Verkhoyansk

Yakutsk

Kara
Chita

Lake Baikal

Verkholensk

Irkutsk

Lena

S O V I E T   U N I O N

Krasnoyarsk

Turukhansk

Yenisei

Yeniseisk
Achinsk

Minusinsk

S I B E R I A

Narym

Tomsk

Ob

TRANS-SIBERIAN RAILWAY

Omsk

Lake Balkhash

Aral Sea

TURKESTAN UNION

Tashkent

NORTHERN UNION

Nizhni Novgorod

URAL UNION

Ufa

St.Petersburg
Tver
Moscow
Pskov

CENTRAL UNION

Penza
Simbirsk
Tambov
Saratov
Samara

VOLGA UNION

Dvinsk
Bialystok
Vitebsk
Smolensk
Gomel
Zhitomir

Warsaw

NORTH WESTERN UNION

UKRAINIAN UNION

Poltava
Ekaterinoslav

Novocherkassk

DON UNION

Stavropol

Caspian Sea

Baku

Tiflis

CAUCASIAN UNION

Kishinev

SOUTHERN UNION

Odessa

Sebastopol

Black Sea

0   500
Miles

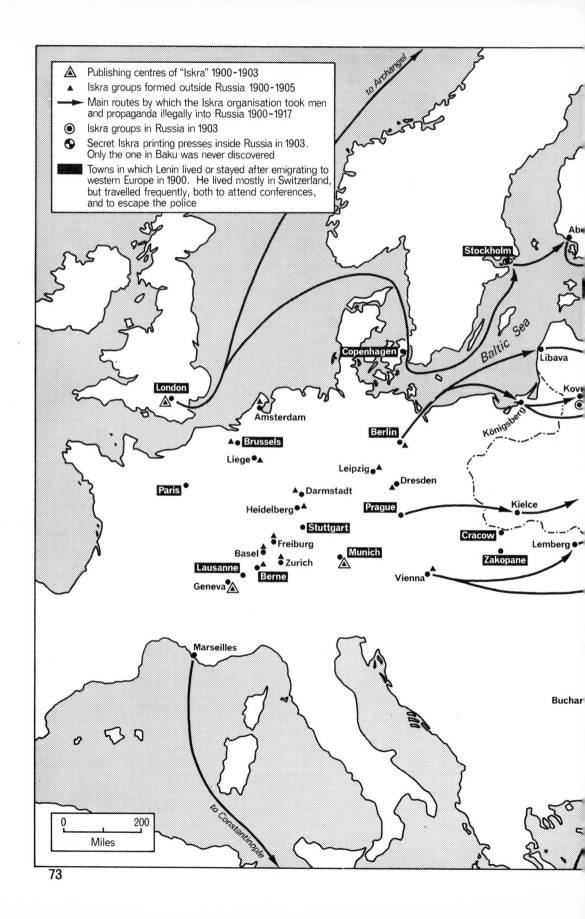

Legend:

⚠ Publishing centres of "Iskra" 1900-1903

▲ Iskra groups formed outside Russia 1900-1905

➡ Main routes by which the Iskra organisation took men and propaganda illegally into Russia 1900-1917

◉ Iskra groups in Russia in 1903

◒ Secret Iskra printing presses inside Russia in 1903. Only the one in Baku was never discovered

■ Towns in which Lenin lived or stayed after emigrating to western Europe in 1900. He lived mostly in Switzerland, but travelled frequently, both to attend conferences, and to escape the police

Map labels:

to Archangel

Stockholm

Abo

Baltic Sea

Copenhagen

Libava

Kov

London

Königsberg

Amsterdam

Berlin

Brussels

Liége

Leipzig

Dresden

Paris

Darmstadt

Kielce

Heidelberg

Prague

Stuttgart

Cracow

Lemberg

Freiburg

Basel

Zurich

Munich

Zakopane

Lausanne

Berne

Vienna

Geneva

Marseilles

Buchar

to Constantinople

0   200
Miles

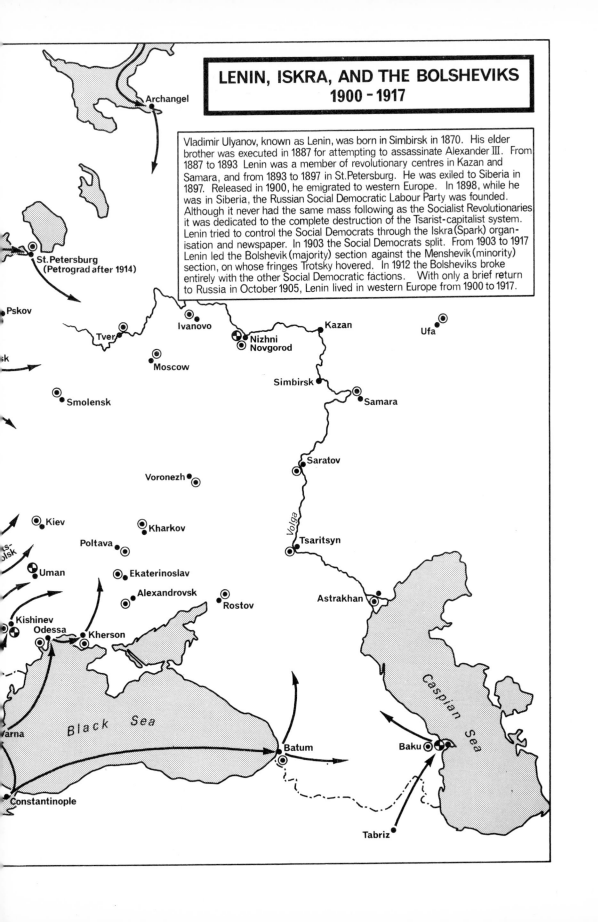

LENIN, ISKRA, AND THE BOLSHEVIKS 1900 - 1917

Vladimir Ulyanov, known as Lenin, was born in Simbirsk in 1870. His elder brother was executed in 1887 for attempting to assassinate Alexander III. From 1887 to 1893 Lenin was a member of revolutionary centres in Kazan and Samara, and from 1893 to 1897 in St.Petersburg. He was exiled to Siberia in 1897. Released in 1900, he emigrated to western Europe. In 1898, while he was in Siberia, the Russian Social Democratic Labour Party was founded. Although it never had the same mass following as the Socialist Revolutionaries it was dedicated to the complete destruction of the Tsarist-capitalist system. Lenin tried to control the Social Democrats through the Iskra (Spark) organisation and newspaper. In 1903 the Social Democrats split. From 1903 to 1917 Lenin led the Bolshevik (majority) section against the Menshevik (minority) section, on whose fringes Trotsky hovered. In 1912 the Bolsheviks broke entirely with the other Social Democratic factions. With only a brief return to Russia in October 1905, Lenin lived in western Europe from 1900 to 1917.

Archangel

St. Petersburg
(Petrograd after 1914)

Pskov

Tver

Ivanovo

Nizhni
Novgorod

Kazan

Ufa

Moscow

Simbirsk

Samara

Smolensk

Saratov

Voronezh

Volga

Kiev

Kharkov

Poltava

Tsaritsyn

Uman

Ekaterinoslav

Alexandrovsk

Rostov

Astrakhan

Kishinev
Odessa

Kherson

Caspian Sea

Varna

Black Sea

Batum

Baku

Constantinople

Tabriz

THE PROVINCES AND POPULATION OF EUROPEAN RUSSIA IN 1900

NORWAY

SWEDEN

GERMANY

POLISH PROVINCES

AUSTRIA-HUNGARY

RUMANIA

TURKEY

PERSIA

White Sea

Baltic Sea

Black Sea

Caspian Sea

ARCHANGEL

FINLAND

OLONETS

VOLOGDA

PERM

ESTLAND

ST PETERSBURG

NOVGOROD

KOSTROMA

VIATKA

KURLAND

LIVLAND

PSKOV

YAROSLAVL

TVER

KURLAND

KOVNO

VITEBSK

VLADIMIR

NIZHNI NOVGOROD

KAZAN

UFA

VILNA

MOSCOW

SMOLENSK

KALUGA

SIMBIRSK

GRODNO

MOGILEV

TULA

PENZA

ORENBURG

MINSK

OREL

RIAZAN

SAMARA

VOLHYNIA

CHERNIGOV

KURSK

TAMBOV

SARATOV

KIEV

POLTAVA

VORONEZH

PODOLIA

KHARKOV

BESSARABIA

KHERSON

EKATERINOSLAV

DON

ASTRAKHAN

TAURIDA

KUBAN

STAVROPOL

TEREK

TRANS-CAUCASIAN PROVINCES

The first official Russian census was held in 1897. The total population was just over 129 million - nearly as large as the combined populations of Britain, France, and Germany. Over 80% of all Russians were peasants. Finland was an autonomous Duchy, and, like Poland, was subdivided into Provinces

MAIN NATIONAL & ETHNIC GROUPS IN EUROPEAN RUSSIA IN 1900	
Russians	55 million
Ukrainians	22 million
Poles	8 million
White Russians	6 million
Jews	5 million
Balts	4 million
Caucasians	3 million
Germans	2 million

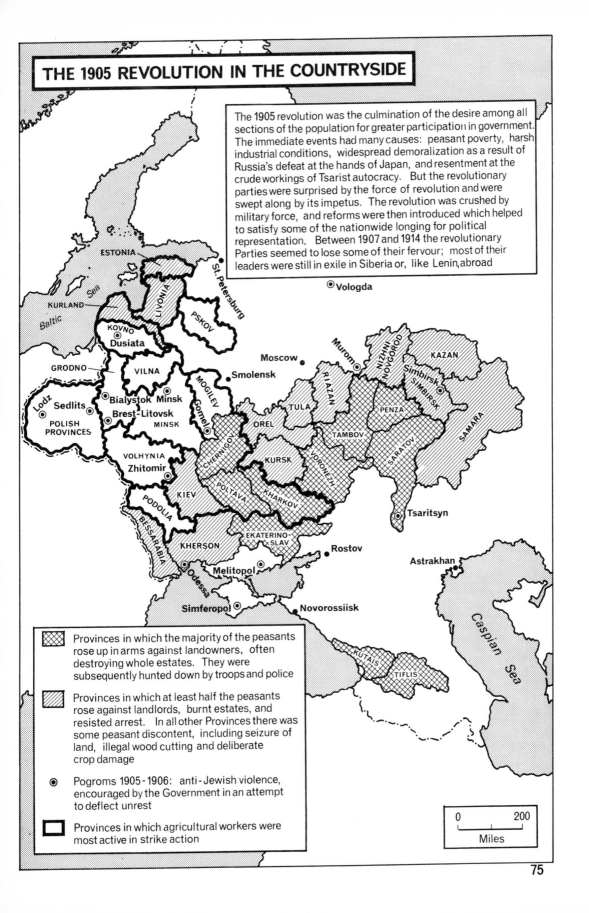

THE 1905 REVOLUTION IN THE COUNTRYSIDE

The 1905 revolution was the culmination of the desire among all sections of the population for greater participation in government. The immediate events had many causes: peasant poverty, harsh industrial conditions, widespread demoralization as a result of Russia's defeat at the hands of Japan, and resentment at the crude workings of Tsarist autocracy. But the revolutionary parties were surprised by the force of revolution and were swept along by its impetus. The revolution was crushed by military force, and reforms were then introduced which helped to satisfy some of the nationwide longing for political representation. Between 1907 and 1914 the revolutionary Parties seemed to lose some of their fervour; most of their leaders were still in exile in Siberia or, like Lenin, abroad

ESTONIA

KURLAND

LIVONIA

Baltic Sea

St. Petersburg

⊙ Vologda

KOVNO
Dusiata

PSKOV

Moscow

Murom

NIZHNI NOVGOROD

KAZAN

GRODNO

VILNA

Smolensk

MOGILEV

Simbirsk

SIMBIRSK

Lodz
Sedlits

Bialystok Minsk
Brest-Litovsk

MINSK

Gomel

OREL

TULA

RIAZAN

PENZA

POLISH PROVINCES

VOLHYNIA
Zhitomir

CHERNIGOV

KURSK

TAMBOV

VORONEZH

SARATOV

SAMARA

KIEV

POLTAVA

PODOLIA

KHARKOV

Tsaritsyn

BESSARABIA

KHERSON

EKATERINO-SLAV

Rostov

Astrakhan

Odessa

Melitopol

Novorossiisk

Simferopol

Caspian Sea

KUTAIS

TIFLIS

Provinces in which the majority of the peasants rose up in arms against landowners, often destroying whole estates. They were subsequently hunted down by troops and police

Provinces in which at least half the peasants rose against landlords, burnt estates, and resisted arrest. In all other Provinces there was some peasant discontent, including seizure of land, illegal wood cutting and deliberate crop damage

⊙ Pogroms 1905-1906: anti-Jewish violence, encouraged by the Government in an attempt to deflect unrest

Provinces in which agricultural workers were most active in strike action

0   200
Miles

75

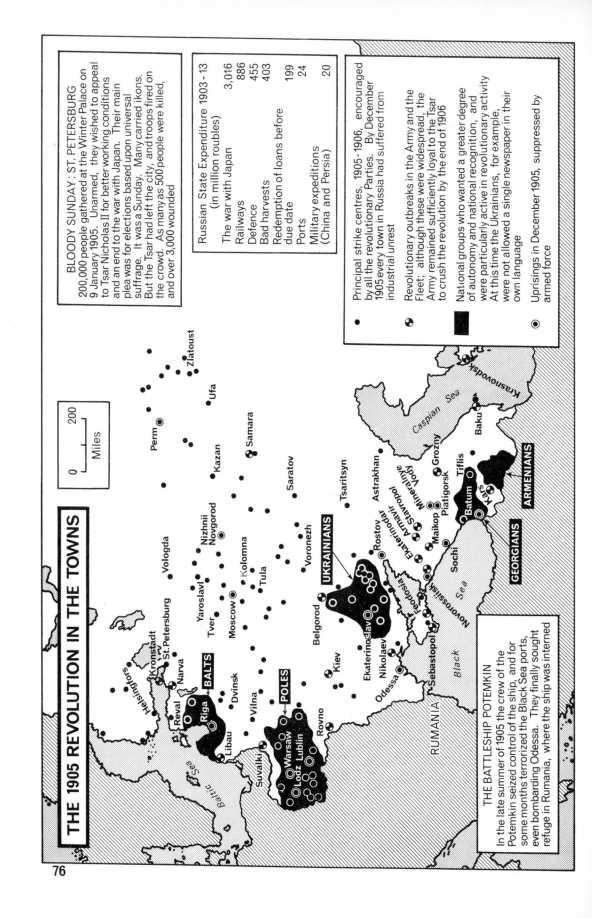

THE 1905 REVOLUTION IN THE TOWNS

BLOODY SUNDAY : ST. PETERSBURG

200,000 people gathered at the Winter Palace on 9 January 1905. Unarmed, they wished to appeal to Tsar Nicholas II for better working conditions and an end to the war with Japan. Their main plea was for elections based upon universal suffrage. It was a Sunday. Many carried ikons. But the Tsar had left the city, and troops fired on the crowd. As many as 500 people were killed, and over 3,000 wounded

Russian State Expenditure 1903 - 13 (in million roubles)	
The war with Japan	3,016
Railways	886
Defence	455
Bad harvests	403
Redemption of loans before due date	199
Ports	24
Military expeditions (China and Persia)	20

- Principal strike centres, 1905-1906, encouraged by all the revolutionary Parties. By December 1905 every town in Russia had suffered from industrial unrest

- Revolutionary outbreaks in the Army and the Fleet; although these were widespread, the Army remained sufficiently loyal to the Tsar to crush the revolution by the end of 1906

- National groups who wanted a greater degree of autonomy and national recognition, and were particularly active in revolutionary activity. At this time the Ukrainians, for example, were not allowed a single newspaper in their own language

- Uprisings in December 1905, suppressed by armed force

THE BATTLESHIP POTEMKIN

In the late summer of 1905 the crew of the Potemkin seized control of the ship, and for some months terrorized the Black Sea ports, even bombarding Odessa. They finally sought refuge in Rumania, where the ship was interned

BALTS

POLES

UKRAINIANS

GEORGIANS

ARMENIANS

0 — 200 Miles

Zlatoust · Ufa · Perm · Samara · Kazan · Saratov · Tsaritsyn · Astrakhan · Vologda · Nizhnii Novgorod · Kolomna · Tula · Voronezh · Yaroslavl · Tver · Moscow · Belgorod · Rostov · Ekaterinodar · Ekaterinoslav · Nikolaev · Odessa · Kiev · Rovno · Lublin · Lodz · Warsaw · Suvalki · Vilna · Dvinsk · Libau · Riga · Reval · Narva · St. Petersburg · Kronstadt · Helsingfors · Sebastopol · Feodosia · Novorossiisk · Sochi · Batum · Tiflis · Kars · Grozny · Piatigorsk · Maikop · Stavropol · Mineralnye Vody · Armavir · Baku · Krasnovodsk

RUMANIA

Black Sea · Caspian Sea · Baltic Sea

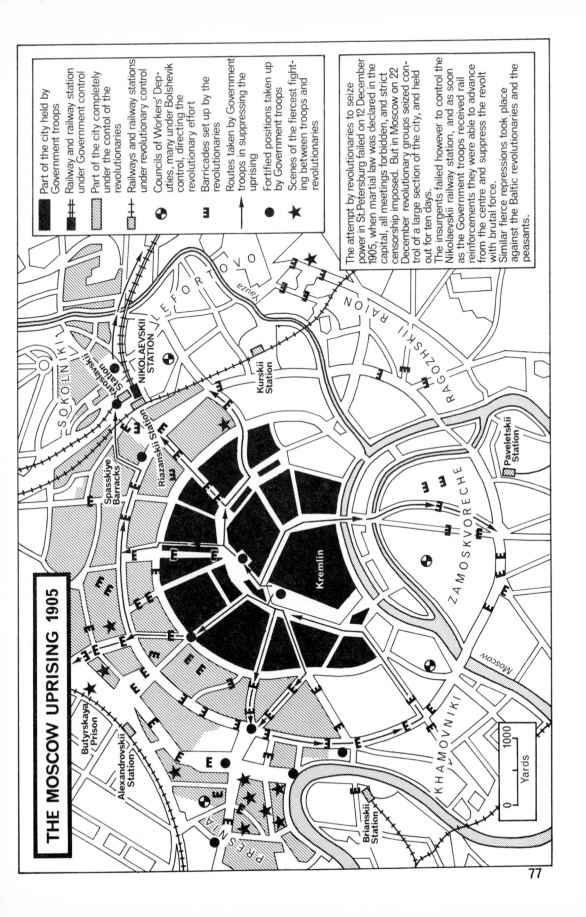

THE MOSCOW UPRISING 1905

Legend

- ■ Part of the city held by Government troops
- ## Railway and railway station under Government control
- ▨ Part of the city completely under the control of the revolutionaries
- ◫+ Railways and railway stations under revolutionary control
- ◕ Councils of Workers' Deputies, many under Bolshevik control, directing the revolutionary effort
- Ε Barricades set up by the revolutionaries
- ↑ Routes taken by Government troops in suppressing the uprising
- ● Fortified positions taken up by Government troops
- ★ Scenes of the fiercest fighting between troops and revolutionaries

The attempt by revolutionaries to seize power in St.Petersburg failed on 12 December 1905, when martial law was declared in the capital, all meetings forbidden, and strict censorship imposed. But in Moscow on 22 December revolutionary groups seized control of a large section of the city, and held out for ten days.

The insurgents failed however to control the Nikolaevskii railway station, and as soon as the Government troops received rail reinforcements they were able to advance from the centre and suppress the revolt with brutal force.

Similar fierce repressions took place against the Baltic revolutionaries and the peasants.

LEFORTOVO

Yauza

SOKOLNIKI

Yaroslavskii Station

NIKOLAEVSKII STATION

Kurskii Station

RAGOZHSKII RAION

Spasskiye Barracks

Riazanskii Station

Paveletskii Station

ZAMOSKVORECHE

Kremlin

Moscow

Butyrskaya Prison

Alexandrovskii Station

KHAMOVNIKI

P R E S N Y A

Brianskii Station

0   1000
Yards

77

RUSSIA AND THE BALKANS 1876-1885

Russia wanted to drive the Turk from Europe and dominate the Balkans. Britain supported Russian protests against Turkish atrocities against the Bulgarians in 1875, which led Russia to attack Turkey. After defeating the Turks at Plevna in 1876 Russia tried to set up a large independent Bulgaria, but Britain and Austria-Hungary challenged Russia's aspirations, and under German mediation Russia agreed to the creation of a much smaller Bulgaria. Austria advanced her own Balkan interests by occupying the former Turkish province of Bosnia, which she formally annexed in 1908, and entering Novi Pazar.

0   100

Miles

RUSSIA

AUSTRIA—HUNGARY

R U M A N I A

BOSNIA

Belgrade

Bucharest

Constanza

Sarajevo

SERBIA

Danube

Black Sea

NOVI PAZAR

Plevna

Silistria

B U L G A R I A

Varna

Nish

Tirnovo

Adriatic Sea

Cattaro

Sofia

Burgas

MONTENEGRO

EAST RUMELIA

Midia

Skopje

Adrianople

Constantinople

MACEDONIA

Kavalla

Rodosto

San Stephano

Dedeagatch

Chanak

Aegean Sea

TURKEY – IN – ASIA

G R E E C E

Athens

- ·— The boundary of Turkey-in-Europe 1876

- ☐ Russian proposal for an independent "Big Bulgaria", agreed to by the Turks at the Treaty of San Stephano 1878

- ■ Bulgaria, autonomous, not independent, as allowed by Britain and Germany by the Treaty of Berlin 1878

- Turkish territory added to Serbia, Rumania and Montenegro (who each gained their independence from Turkey) by the Treaty of Berlin 1878; and to Greece in 1881

- Occupied by Austria-Hungary in 1878

- Added to Bulgaria in 1885, when Bulgaria became fully independent of Turkey

78

RUSSIA, THE BALKANS, AND THE COMING OF WAR 1912-1914

0   500

Miles

North
Sea

BRITAIN

St. Petersburg

Reval

Baltic Sea

Riga

BALTIC PROVINCES

Moscow

RUSSIA

Danzig

Berlin

Warsaw

Pripet
Marshes

POLISH
PROVINCES

Kiev

GERMANY

Breslau

VOLHYNIA

Paris

Lemberg

FRANCE

Vienna

Budapest

AUSTRIA - HUNGARY

BOSNIA

Sarajevo

Belgrade

RUMANIA

Black Sea

SERBIA

Adriatic Sea

BULGARIA

Constantinople

MONTENEGRO

ALBANIA

Skopje

Bosphorus

GREECE

Dardanelles

TURKEY

Russia's mid-century alignment with
Germany was changed during the 1880's
to a new alignment with France,
while at the same time Austria and
Germany drew closer together. In the
two Balkan Wars of 1912 and 1913
Turkey was driven almost entirely
from Europe, but Russia's position
did not improve; for as a result of
Turkey's defeat Austrian influence
increased even further. In June 1914
a Bosnian Serb murdered the Austrian
heir to the throne, Archduke Franz-
Ferdinand, at Sarajevo. Austria
invaded Serbia on 28 July 1914.
Russia then declared war on Austria.
Germany supported her ally Austria
and declared war on Russia. France
and Britain joined Russia against
Germany and Austria. Turkey
attacked Russia in October 1914

Countries in which Austrian and German influence
worked against Russia. Greece had a pro-German
King; Turkey a pro-German Minister of War and
virtual dictator; Bulgaria and Rumania had both
accepted alliance with the Central Powers

Area of Russia in which Germany hoped to expand
as a result of war

Russia's only two Balkan Allies, both threatened by
Austria. Austria had created the state of Albania in
1912 in order to cut Serbia off from the sea.

Countries in western Europe sympathetic to Russia.
France had a military alliance with Russia dating from
1894. Britain a convention dating from 1907

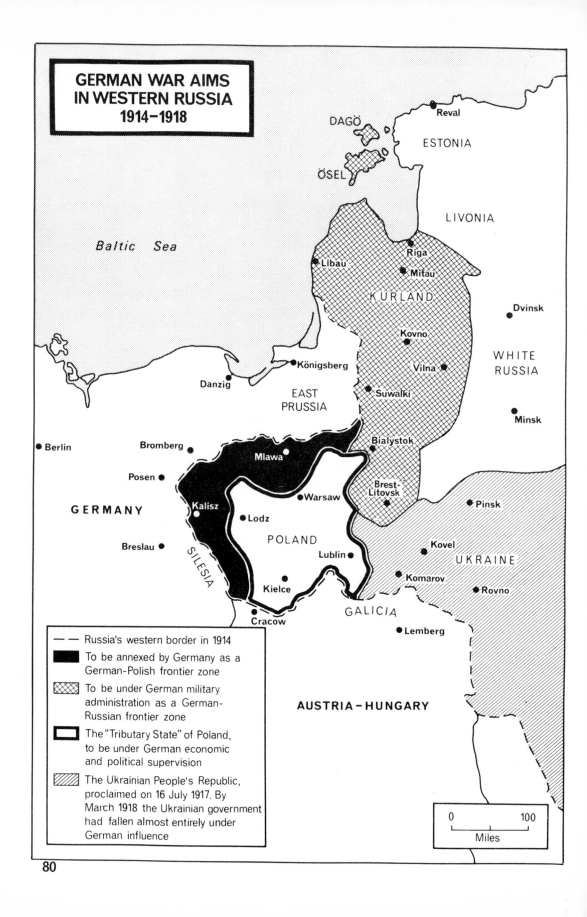

GERMAN WAR AIMS IN WESTERN RUSSIA 1914–1918

Baltic Sea

DAGÖ

ÖSEL

● Reval

ESTONIA

LIVONIA

● Riga

● Libau

● Mitau

KURLAND

● Dvinsk

● Kovno

WHITE RUSSIA

● Vilna

● Königsberg

● Danzig

EAST PRUSSIA

● Suwalki

● Minsk

● Bialystok

● Berlin

● Bromberg

● Mlawa

● Posen

Brest-Litovsk

● Pinsk

GERMANY

● Kalisz

● Warsaw

● Lodz

● Breslau

POLAND

● Kovel

UKRAINE

SILESIA

● Lublin

● Komarov

● Kielce

● Rovno

● Cracow

GALICIA

● Lemberg

Russia's western border in 1914

To be annexed by Germany as a German-Polish frontier zone

To be under German military administration as a German-Russian frontier zone

The "Tributary State" of Poland, to be under German economic and political supervision

The Ukrainian People's Republic, proclaimed on 16 July 1917. By March 1918 the Ukrainian government had fallen almost entirely under German influence

AUSTRIA – HUNGARY

0   100

Miles

80

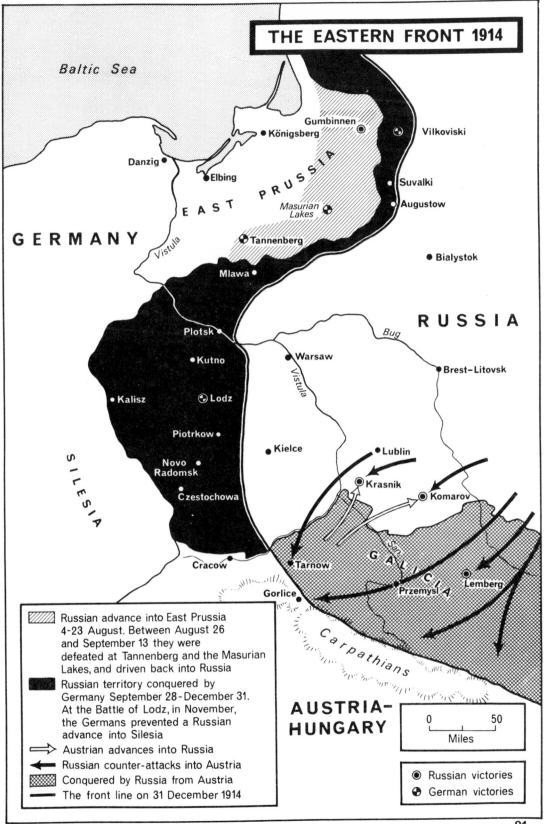

THE EASTERN FRONT 1914

Baltic Sea

GERMANY

EAST PRUSSIA

Vistula

RUSSIA

- Danzig
- Elbing
- Königsberg
- Gumbinnen
- Vilkoviski
- Suvalki
- Augustow
- *Masurian Lakes*
- Tannenberg
- Mlawa
- Bialystok
- Plotsk
- Kutno
- Warsaw
- *Bug*
- Brest–Litovsk
- Kalisz
- Lodz
- *Vistula*
- Piotrkow
- Kielce
- Novo Radomsk
- Lublin
- Czestochowa
- Krasnik
- Komarov
- **SILESIA**
- Cracow
- Tarnow
- *San*
- **GALICIA**
- Gorlice
- Przemysl
- Lemberg
- *Carpathians*

AUSTRIA-HUNGARY

Russian advance into East Prussia 4-23 August. Between August 26 and September 13 they were defeated at Tannenberg and the Masurian Lakes, and driven back into Russia

Russian territory conquered by Germany September 28-December 31. At the Battle of Lodz, in November, the Germans prevented a Russian advance into Silesia

⇨ Austrian advances into Russia

← Russian counter-attacks into Austria

Conquered by Russia from Austria

— The front line on 31 December 1914

0   50
Miles

⊙ Russian victories
⊕ German victories

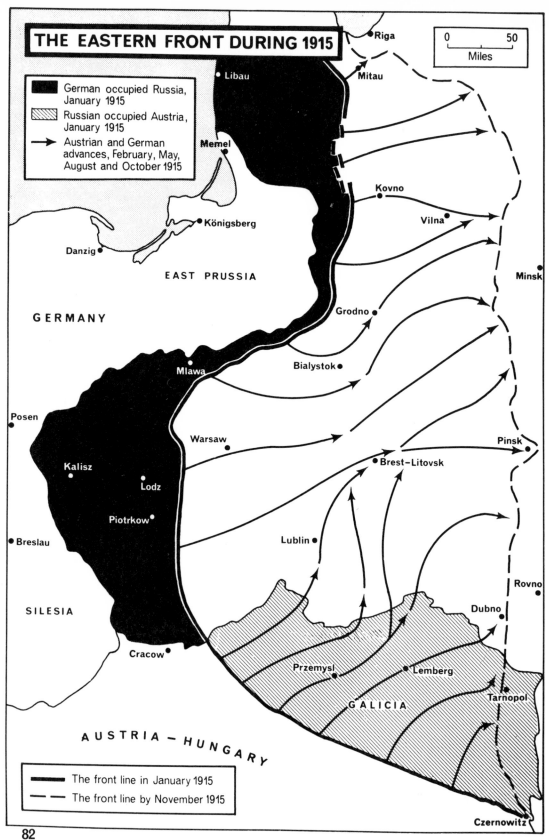

THE EASTERN FRONT DURING 1915

Legend:
- German occupied Russia, January 1915
- Russian occupied Austria, January 1915
- → Austrian and German advances, February, May, August and October 1915

Scale: 0 — 50 Miles

Riga

Libau

Mitau

Memel

Kovno

Königsberg

Vilna

Danzig

EAST PRUSSIA

Minsk

GERMANY

Grodno

Mlawa

Bialystok

Posen

Warsaw

Pinsk

Kalisz

Lodz

Brest–Litovsk

Piotrkow

Breslau

Lublin

Rovno

SILESIA

Dubno

Cracow

Przemysl

Lemberg

GALICIA

Tarnopol

AUSTRIA – HUNGARY

The front line in January 1915

- - - The front line by November 1915

Czernowitz

82

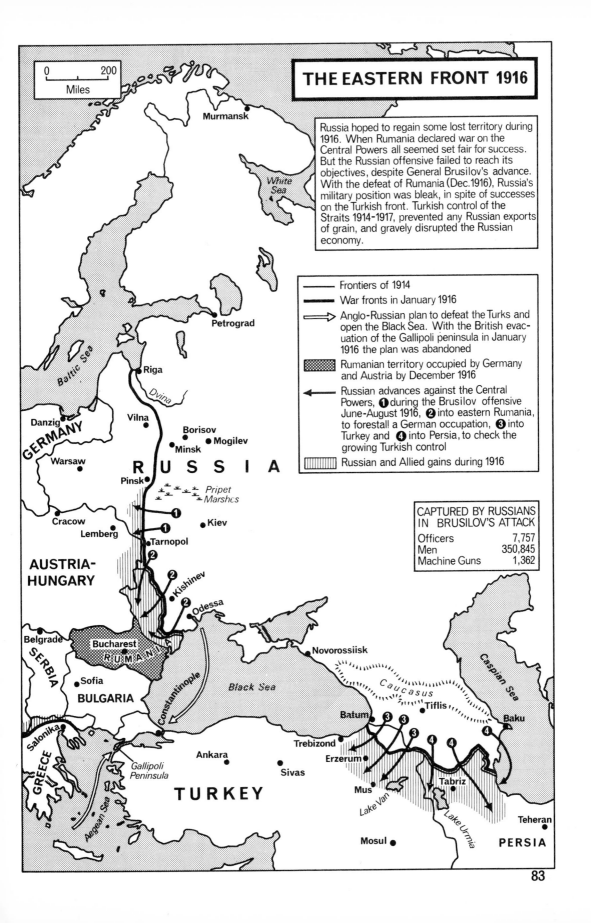

THE EASTERN FRONT 1916

Russia hoped to regain some lost territory during 1916. When Rumania declared war on the Central Powers all seemed set fair for success. But the Russian offensive failed to reach its objectives, despite General Brusilov's advance. With the defeat of Rumania (Dec.1916), Russia's military position was bleak, in spite of successes on the Turkish front. Turkish control of the Straits 1914-1917, prevented any Russian exports of grain, and gravely disrupted the Russian economy.

Frontiers of 1914

War fronts in January 1916

Anglo-Russian plan to defeat the Turks and open the Black Sea. With the British evacuation of the Gallipoli peninsula in January 1916 the plan was abandoned

Rumanian territory occupied by Germany and Austria by December 1916

Russian advances against the Central Powers, ❶ during the Brusilov offensive June-August 1916, ❷ into eastern Rumania, to forestall a German occupation, ❸ into Turkey and ❹ into Persia, to check the growing Turkish control

Russian and Allied gains during 1916

CAPTURED BY RUSSIANS IN BRUSILOV'S ATTACK

Officers	7,757
Men	350,845
Machine Guns	1,362

83

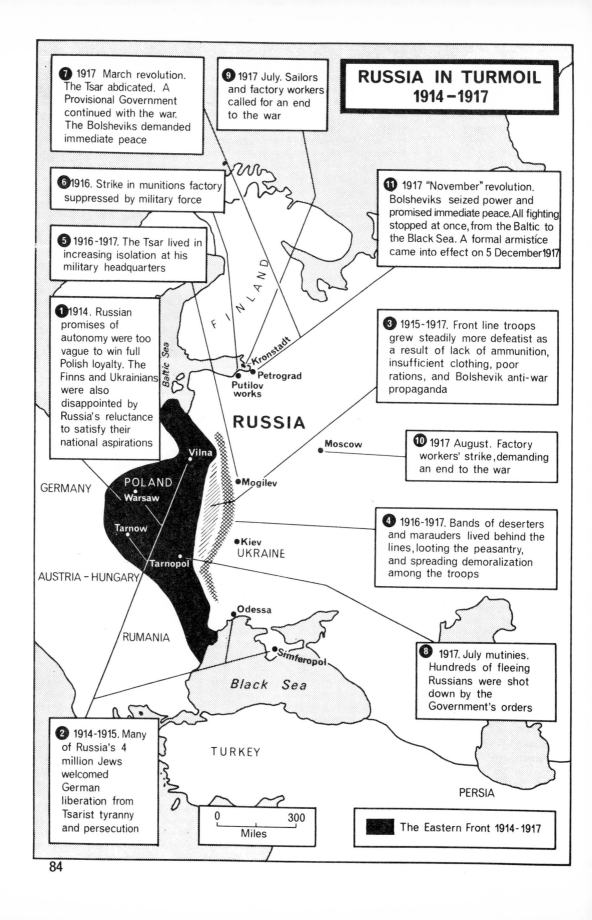

RUSSIA IN TURMOIL 1914-1917

7 1917 March revolution. The Tsar abdicated. A Provisional Government continued with the war. The Bolsheviks demanded immediate peace

9 1917 July. Sailors and factory workers called for an end to the war

6 1916. Strike in munitions factory suppressed by military force

5 1916-1917. The Tsar lived in increasing isolation at his military headquarters

1 1914. Russian promises of autonomy were too vague to win full Polish loyalty. The Finns and Ukrainians were also disappointed by Russia's reluctance to satisfy their national aspirations

11 1917 "November" revolution. Bolsheviks seized power and promised immediate peace. All fighting stopped at once, from the Baltic to the Black Sea. A formal armistice came into effect on 5 December 1917

3 1915-1917. Front line troops grew steadily more defeatist as a result of lack of ammunition, insufficient clothing, poor rations, and Bolshevik anti-war propaganda

10 1917 August. Factory workers' strike, demanding an end to the war

4 1916-1917. Bands of deserters and marauders lived behind the lines, looting the peasantry, and spreading demoralization among the troops

8 1917. July mutinies. Hundreds of fleeing Russians were shot down by the Government's orders

2 1914-1915. Many of Russia's 4 million Jews welcomed German liberation from Tsarist tyranny and persecution

FINLAND

Kronstadt
Petrograd
Putilov works

RUSSIA

Moscow

Vilna

POLAND
Warsaw

Mogilev

Tarnow

Tarnopol

Kiev
UKRAINE

GERMANY

AUSTRIA – HUNGARY

RUMANIA

Odessa

Simferopol

Black Sea

TURKEY

PERSIA

Baltic Sea

0   300
Miles

■ The Eastern Front 1914-1917

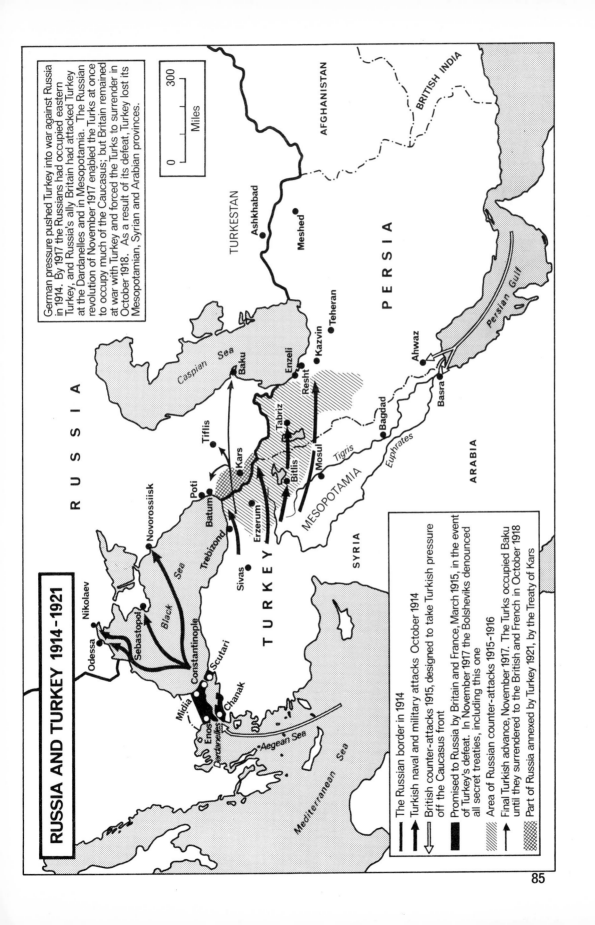

RUSSIA AND TURKEY 1914–1921

German pressure pushed Turkey into war against Russia in 1914. By 1917 the Russians had occupied eastern Turkey, and Russia's ally Britain had attacked Turkey at the Dardanelles and in Mesopotamia. The Russian revolution of November 1917 enabled the Turks at once to occupy much of the Caucasus; but Britain remained at war with Turkey and forced the Turks to surrender in October 1918. As a result of its defeat, Turkey lost its Mesopotamian, Syrian and Arabian provinces.

300

Miles

0

AFGHANISTAN

BRITISH INDIA

TURKESTAN

Ashkhabad

Meshed

P E R S I A

Teheran

Kazvin

Caspian Sea

Baku

Enzeli

Resht

Tabriz

Ahwaz

Persian Gulf

Basra

Bagdad

Tigris

Euphrates

Mosul

MESOPOTAMIA

ARABIA

Tiflis

Kars

Bitlis

Erzerum

R U S S I A

Poti

Batum

Trebizond

Novorossiisk

Sivas

Black Sea

SYRIA

Nikolaev

Sebastopol

T U R K E Y

Odessa

Constantinople

Scutari

Chanak

Midia

Enos

Dardanelles

Aegean Sea

Mediterranean Sea

The Russian border in 1914

Turkish naval and military attacks October 1914

British counter-attacks 1915, designed to take Turkish pressure off the Caucasus front

Promised to Russia by Britain and France, March 1915, in the event of Turkey's defeat. In November 1917 the Bolsheviks denounced all secret treaties, including this one

Area of Russian counter-attacks 1915–1916

Final Turkish advance, November 1917. The Turks occupied Baku until they surrendered to the British and French in October 1918

Part of Russia annexed by Turkey 1921, by the Treaty of Kars

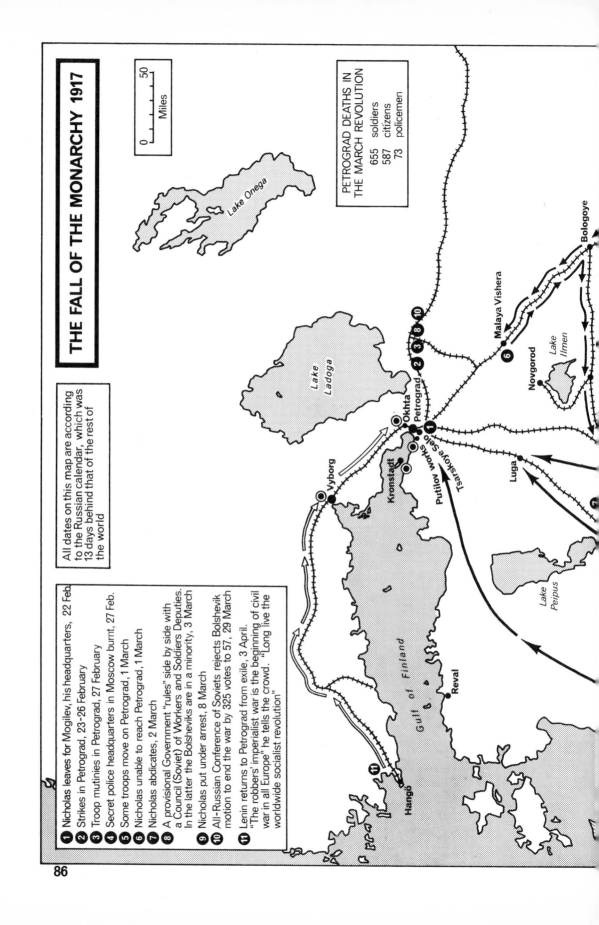

THE FALL OF THE MONARCHY 1917

0 50
Miles

All dates on this map are according to the Russian calendar, which was 13 days behind that of the rest of the world

PETROGRAD DEATHS IN THE MARCH REVOLUTION
655 soldiers
587 citizens
73 policemen

1. Nicholas leaves for Mogilev, his headquarters, 22 Feb.
2. Strikes in Petrograd, 23-26 February
3. Troop mutinies in Petrograd, 27 February
4. Secret police headquarters in Moscow burnt, 27 Feb.
5. Some troops move on Petrograd, 1 March
6. Nicholas unable to reach Petrograd, 1 March
7. Nicholas abdicates, 2 March
8. A provisional Government "rules" side by side with a Council (Soviet) of Workers and Soldiers Deputies. In the latter the Bolsheviks are in a minority, 3 March
9. Nicholas put under arrest, 8 March
10. All-Russian Conference of Soviets rejects Bolshevik motion to end the war by 325 votes to 57, 29 March
11. Lenin returns to Petrograd from exile, 3 April. "The robbers' imperialist war is the beginning of civil war in all Europe" he tells the crowd. "Long live the worldwide socialist revolution"

Lake Onega

Lake Ladoga

Lake Ilmen

Lake Peipus

Gulf of Finland

Hangö

Reval

Vyborg

Kronstadt

Okhta
Petrograd
Putilov Works
Tsarskoye Selo

Novgorod

Malaya Vishera

Bologoye

Luga

86

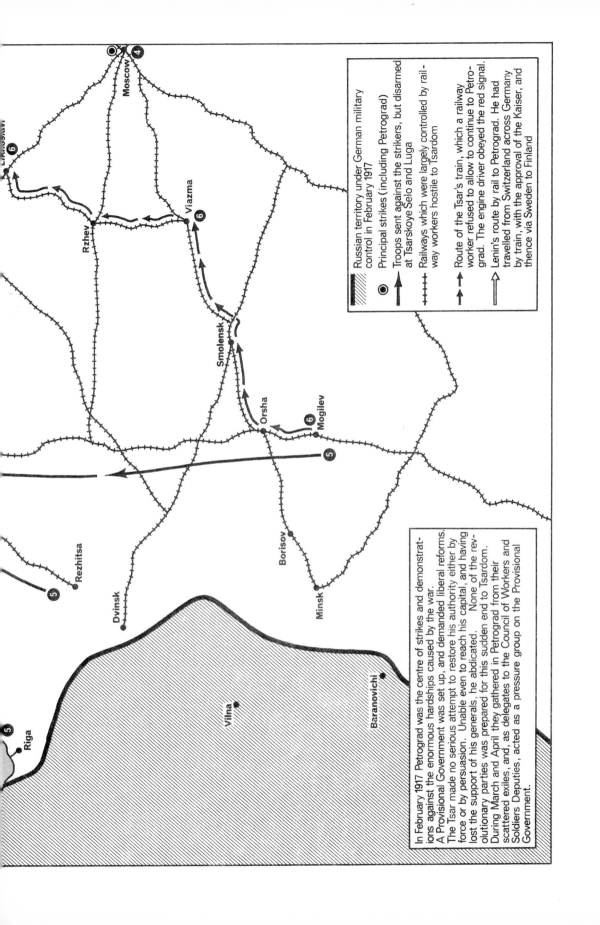

Legend:

- ⬛ (hatched) Russian territory under German military control in February 1917
- ⦿ Principal strikes (including Petrograd)
- ⬆ Troops sent against the strikers, but disarmed at TsarskoyeSelo and Luga
- ⊢⊢⊢ Railways which were largely controlled by railway workers hostile to Tsardom
- ↑↑ Route of the Tsar's train, which a railway worker refused to allow to continue to Petrograd. The engine driver obeyed the red signal.
- ⬆ (open arrow) Lenin's route by rail to Petrograd. He had travelled from Switzerland across Germany by train, with the approval of the Kaiser, and thence via Sweden to Finland

In February 1917 Petrograd was the centre of strikes and demonstrations against the enormous hardships caused by the war. A Provisional Government was set up, and demanded liberal reforms. The Tsar made no serious attempt to restore his authority either by force or by persuasion. Unable even to reach his capital, and having lost the support of his generals, he abdicated. None of the revolutionary parties was prepared for this sudden end to Tsardom. During March and April they gathered in Petrograd from their scattered exiles, and, as delegates to the Council of Workers and Soldiers Deputies, acted as a pressure group on the Provisional Government.

Map labels: Moscow, Rzhev, Viazma, Smolensk, Orsha, Mogilev, Borisov, Minsk, Baranovichi, Vilna, Dvinsk, Rezhitsa, Riga

Numbers shown on map: 4, 5, 6

LENIN'S RETURN TO RUSSIA 1917

Our tactics: absolute distrust; no support of new Government; Kerensky particularly suspect; to arm proletariat only guarantee; no rapprochement with other parties. This last is conditio sine qua non
LENIN TO BOLSHEVIKS IN SWEDEN TELEGRAM FROM BERN 26 MARCH 1917

0   250
Miles

On 7 August 1914 Lenin was arrested in Cracow by the Austrians as an enemy alien and spy. He was released on 23 Aug., the Austrian Government having been persuaded that he was even more an enemy of Tsardom, and could "render great services" to Austria by fomenting anti-Tsarist troubles

When revolution broke out in Petrograd in February 1917, Lenin, the Bolshevik leader, was in Switzerland. Wartime was not conducive to travel, nor did his plan to go through Britain prove possible. Instead, the German Government, eager to see dissension and chaos in Russia, agreed with alacrity to his request to travel across "enemy" territory, and provided him with facilities. Thus Imperial Germany served as a hand-maiden to the Russian revolution of October 1917

■ The Central Powers and their conquests in February 1917

–·– Lenin's route from Austria to Switzerland, 1914

····▸ Lenin's first proposed route back to Russia, which proved impossible for fear of arrest by the British

──▸ Lenin's actual route 9-16 April 1917

▨ Sea routes to Russia closed by Central Power minefields

THE LOCATION OF THE BOLSHEVIK LEADERS DURING THE FIRST REVOLUTION OF 1917

The only Bolshevik leaders, none of them very senior, who happened to be in Petrograd at the time of the February Revolution:
MOLOTOV, STEKLOV, SHLYAPNIKOV, LATSIS, and ZALUTSKI

Pacific Ocean

ALASKA

Bering Strait

Arctic Ocean

North Pole

U.S.A.

CANADA

New York

Halifax

GREENLAND

SIBERIA

Lena

ORDZHONIKIDZE
Pokrovsk

Chita

STALIN
Kureika
Turukhansk
SVERDLOV
Irkutsk

Yenisei

Achinsk
KAMENEV

Ob

Narym
RYKOV

CHINA

New York
BUKHARIN
TROTSKY Ⓜ
VOLODARSKY Ⓜ

Stockholm
KOLLONTAI
URITSKY Ⓜ

London
LITVINOV
CHICHERIN Ⓜ

Paris
ANTONOV-OVSEENKO

SWITZERLAND
LENIN
LUNACHARSKY Ⓜ
RADEK
ZINOVIEV

Atlantic Ocean

SWEDEN

Stockholm

Petrograd

TRANS-SIBERIAN RAILWAY

Urals

Moscow
DZERZHINSKY

London

Paris

FRANCE

SWITZERLAND

TER-PETROSIAN
Kharkov

Jassy
RAKOVSKY

Vladikavkaz
KIROV

Black Sea

PERSIA

Mediterranean Sea

////// Territory controlled by Germany and her allies in March 1917

◎ Centre of the First Russian Revolution, and scene of all subsequent struggles for power during 1917

▬ The location of the Bolshevik leaders at the time of the March Revolution. The majority were in exile or out of Russia. They all made haste to return to Petrograd.

Ⓜ = Mensheviks and others who became Bolsheviks on their return to Petrograd

Most of the Social Democratic leaders of both the Bolshevik and Menshevik factions were abroad or in exile when revolution broke out in Russia in 1917. Those who were in Siberia reached Petrograd early in March, following the spontaneous amnesty of all political prisoners. Also returning in March were those living in Sweden. Next to return, in April, were the "specials" from Switzerland, led by Lenin. Finally, in May, came the "regulars" who had been in Switzerland, or elsewhere abroad.

88

THE WAR AND REVOLUTION JULY AND AUGUST 1917

In March 1917 the Provisional Government assured Britain and France that it would continue the war against the Central Powers. But the offensive launched on 1 July ended two weeks later in mutiny and failure. Mass demonstrations in Petrograd on 16 and 17 July, though leaderless, showed how hated the war had become, and the Bolsheviks soon dominated the Soviets by their cry of "Bread and Peace". The Provisional Government then published evidence of financial dealings between the Bolsheviks and German agents, forced Lenin to go into hiding in Finland, and arrested Trotsky. In August General Kornilov led an army against Petrograd, intending to crush the Soviets and stiffen the Provisional Government against concessions. The Bolsheviks took a leading part in the defence of the city, and greatly increased their military power, having been armed by the Provisional Government. They also gained support among the masses, who feared the return of autocracy

The eastern front on 1 July 1917

Austrian territory conquered by Russia 1 - 16 July 1917

Russian proposals for further offensive action during the second two weeks of July

Subject peoples insisting on independence from Russian rule, and gravely hampering the war effort when their demands were rejected or disregarded

Principal areas of mutiny 17 - 30 July 1917

Kornilov's unsuccessful attack on the capital August 1917

Factory groups between Petrograd and the front with increasingly strong Bolshevik influence July - September 1917

Military units between Petrograd and the front with increasingly strong Bolshevik sections July - September 1917

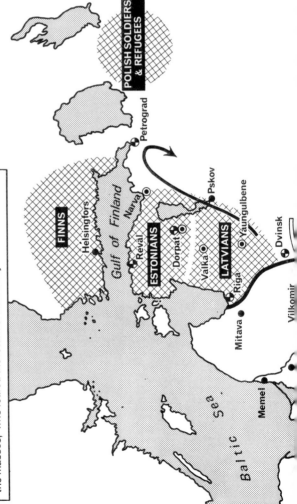

POLISH SOLDIERS & REFUGEES

Petrograd

FINNS

Helsingfors

Gulf of Finland

Narva

Pskov

Reval

ESTONIANS

Dorpat

Valka

Yaungulbene

LATVIANS

Riga

Dvinsk

Mitava

Villkomir

Memel

Baltic Sea

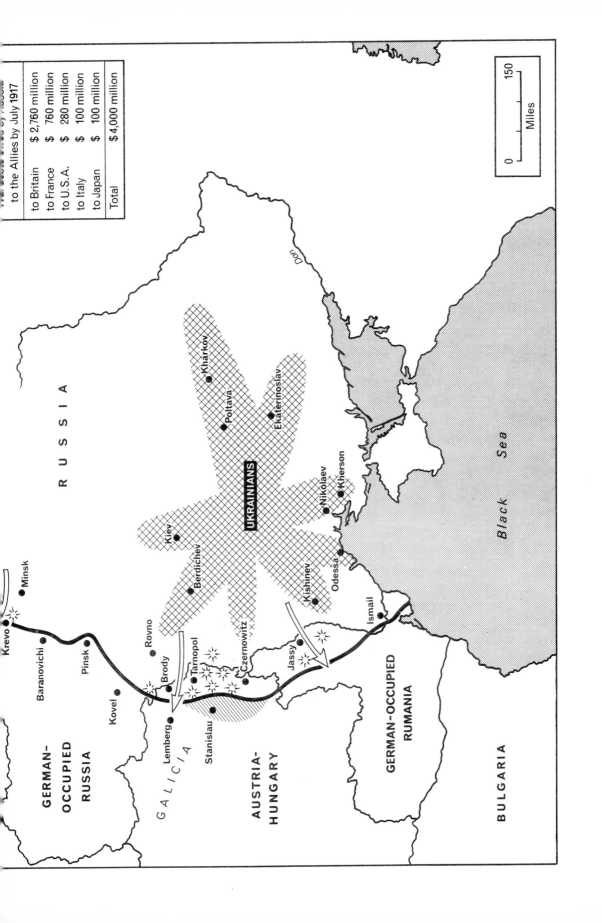

War debt owed by Russia to the Allies by July 1917	
to Britain	$ 2,760 million
to France	$ 760 million
to U.S.A.	$ 280 million
to Italy	$ 100 million
to Japan	$ 100 million
Total	$4,000 million

RUSSIA

GERMAN-OCCUPIED RUSSIA

AUSTRIA-HUNGARY

GALICIA

GERMAN-OCCUPIED RUMANIA

BULGARIA

Black Sea

Don

UKRAINIANS

Krevo
Minsk
Baranovichi
Pinsk
Rovno
Kovel
Brody
Lemberg
Tarnopol
Stanislau
Czernowitz
Jassy
Ismail
Odessa
Kishinev
Kherson
Nikolaev
Berdichev
Kiev
Poltava
Ekaterinoslav
Kharkov

0   150
Miles

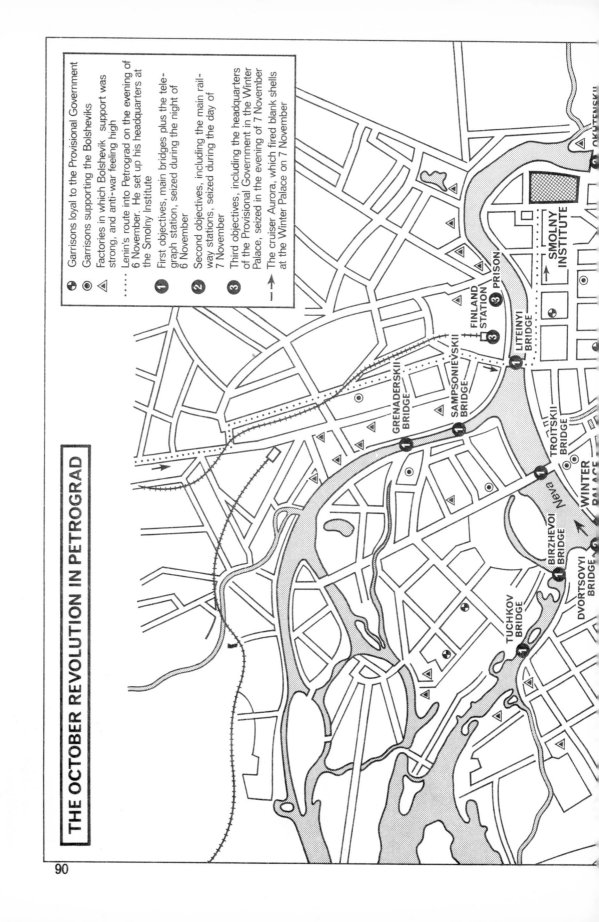

THE OCTOBER REVOLUTION IN PETROGRAD

Garrisons loyal to the Provisional Government

Garrisons supporting the Bolsheviks

Factories in which Bolshevik support was strong, and anti-war feeling high

Lenin's route into Petrograd on the evening of 6 November. He set up his headquarters at the Smolny Institute

1 First objectives, main bridges plus the tele-graph station, seized during the night of 6 November

2 Second objectives, including the main rail-way stations, seized during the day of 7 November

3 Third objectives, including the headquarters of the Provisional Government in the Winter Palace, seized in the evening of 7 November

The cruiser Aurora, which fired blank shells at the Winter Palace on 7 November

SMOLNY INSTITUTE

OKHTENSKII

FINLAND STATION

PRISON

LITEINYI BRIDGE

TROITSKII BRIDGE

WINTER PALACE

SAMPSONIEVSKII BRIDGE

GRENADERSKII BRIDGE

Neva

BIRZHEVOI BRIDGE

DVORTSOVYI BRIDGE

TUCHKOV BRIDGE

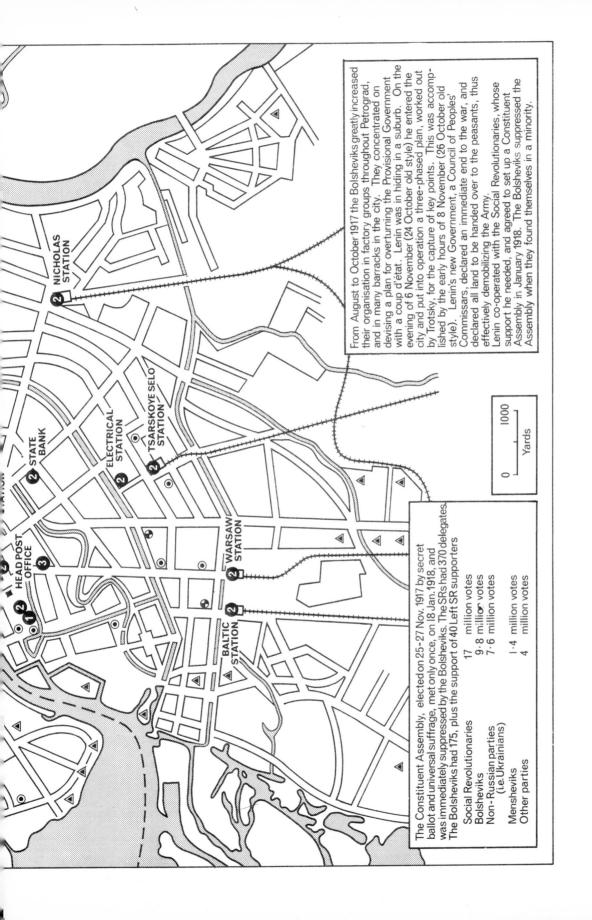

From August to October 1917 the Bolsheviks greatly increased their organisation in factory groups throughout Petrograd, and in many barracks in the city. They concentrated on devising a plan for overturning the Provisional Government with a coup d'état. Lenin was in hiding in a suburb. On the evening of 6 November (24 October old style) he entered the city and put into operation a three-phased plan, worked out by Trotsky, for the capture of key points. This was accomplished by the early hours of 8 November (26 October old style). Lenin's new Government, a Council of Peoples' Commissars, declared an immediate end to the war, and declared all land to be handed over to the peasants, thus effectively demobilizing the Army.
Lenin co-operated with the Social Revolutionaries, whose support he needed, and agreed to set up a Constituent Assembly in January 1918. The Bolsheviks suppressed the Assembly when they found themselves in a minority.

The Constituent Assembly, elected on 25-27 Nov. 1917 by secret ballot and universal suffrage, met only once, on 18 Jan. 1918, and was immediately suppressed by the Bolsheviks. The SRs had 370 delegates. The Bolsheviks had 175, plus the support of 40 Left SR supporters

Social Revolutionaries	17	million votes
Bolsheviks	9·8	million votes
Non-Russian parties	7·6	million votes
(i.e. Ukrainians)		
Mensheviks	1·4	million votes
Other parties	4	million votes

NICHOLAS STATION

STATE BANK

ELECTRICAL STATION

TSARSKOYE SELO STATION

HEAD POST OFFICE

WARSAW STATION

BALTIC STATION

0   1000
Yards

Bibliography of Works Consulted

(i) Atlases

Baratov, R. B. (and others), *Atlas Tadzhikskoi Sovetskoi Sotsialisticheskoi Respubliki* (Dushanbe and Moscow, 1968)

Bartholomew, John (ed), *The Times Atlas of the World*, 5 vols (London, 1959)

Bazilevich, K. V., Golubtsov, I. A. and Zinoviev, M. A., *Atlas Istorii SSSR*, 3 vols (Moscow, 1949–54)

Beloglazova, O. A. (ed), *Atlas SSSR* (Moscow, 1954)

Czaplinski, Wladislaw and Ladogórski, Tadeusz, *Atlas Historyczny Polski* (Warsaw, 1968)

Droysens, G., *Historischer Handatlas* (Bielefeld and Leipzig, 1886)

Durov, A. G. (general editor), *Atlas Leningradskoi Oblasti* (Moscow, 1967)

Engel, Joseph, *Grosser Historischer Weltatlas* (Munich, 1962)

Grosier, L'Abbé, *Atlas Générale de la Chine* (Paris, 1785)

Hudson, G. F. and Rajchman, Marthe, *An Atlas of Far Eastern Politics* (London, 1938)

Kalesnik, S. V. (and others), *Peterburg–Leningrad* (Leningrad, 1957)

Kosev, Dimiter (and others), *Atlas Po Bulgarska Istoriya* (Sofia, 1963)

Kubijovyć, Volodymyr, *Atlas of Ukraine and Adjoining Countries* (Lvov, 1937)

Kudriashov, K. V., *Russkii Istoricheski Atlas* (Leningrad, 1928)

Kovalevsky, Pierre, *Atlas Historique et Culturel de la Russie et du Monde Slave* (Paris, 1961)

McEvedy, Colin, *The Penguin Atlas of Medieval History* (London, 1961)

Penkala, Maria, *A Correlated History of the Far East* (The Hague and Paris, 1966)

Oxford Regional Economic Atlas: The USSR and Eastern Europe (Oxford, 1956)

Sochava, V. B. (principal editor), *Atlas Zabaikalia* (Moscow and Irkutsk, 1967)

Taaffe, Robert N. and Kingsbury, Robert C., *An Atlas of Soviet Affairs* (London, 1965)

Terekhov, N. M. (senior editor), *Atlas Volgogradskoi Oblasti* (Moscow, 1967)

Toynbee, Arnold J. and Myers, Edward D., *Historical Atlas and Gazetteer* (London, 1959)

Voznesenski (and others), *Atlas Razvitiya Khoziastva i Kultury SSSR* (Moscow, 1967)

Westermann, Georg, *Atlas zur Weltgeschichte* (Braunschweig, 1956)

Zamyslovski, Igor E., *Uchebnii Atlas po Russkoi Istorii* (St Petersburg, 1887)

(ii) Maps

Atanasiu, A. D., *La Bessarabie* (Paris, 1919)

Bazewicz, J. M., *Polska w Trzech Zaborach* (Warsaw, n.d.)

Bazileva, Z. P., *Rossiiskaya Imperia 1801–1861* (Moscow, 1960)

British G.H.Q., Constantinople, *Ethnographical Map of Caucasus* (Constantinople, 1920)

Fedorovskaya, G. P. (publisher), *Promyshlennost Rossii 1913, Promyshlennost Soyuza SSR 1940* (Moscow, 1962)

Filonenko, W. J., *Volkstumkarte der Krim* (Vienna, 1932)

Kuchborskaya, E. P., *Rossiiskaya Imperia 1725–1801* (Moscow, 1959)

Stanford, Edward, *Sketch of the Acquisitions of Russia* (London, 1876)

Wyld, James, *Wyld's Military Staff Map of Central Asia, Turkistan and Afghanistan* (London, 1878)

(iii) Encyclopaedias, Reference Books and General Works

Baedeker, Karl, *Russland* (Leipzig, 1912)

Cole, J. P., *Geography of the USSR* (London, 1967)

Florinsky, Michael T. (ed), *Encyclopaedia of Russia and the Soviet Union* (New York, 1961)

Katzenelson, Y. L. and Gintsburg, D. G. (eds), *Evreiskaya Entisiklopediya*, 16 vols (St Petersburg, 1906–13)

Kubijovyć, Volodymyr (ed), *Ukraine: A Concise Encyclopaedia* (Toronto, 1963)

Pares, Bernard, *A History of Russia* (London, 1926)

Parker, W. H., *An Historical Geography of Russia* (London, 1968)

Sumner, B. H., *Survey of Russian History* (London, 1944)

Utechin, S. V., *Everyman's Concise Encyclopaedia of Russia* (London, 1961)

Zhukov, E. M. (ed), *Sovetskaya Istoricheskaya Entisiklopediya*, vols 1–12 (Moscow, 1961–9)

(iv) Books on Special Subjects

Allen, W. E. D., *The Ukraine: A History* (Cambridge, 1940)

Allen, W. E. D. and Muratov, P., *Caucasian Battlefields: A History of the Wars on the Turco-Caucasian Border 1828–1921* (London, 1953)

Allilueva, A. S., *Iz Vospominanii* (Moscow, 1946)

Armstrong, John A. (ed), *Soviet Partisans in World War II* (Madison, 1964)

Armstrong, Terence E., *The Northern Sea Route* (Cambridge, 1952)

Avalishvili, Zourab, *The Independence of Georgia in International Politics 1918–1921* (London, 1940)

Baddeley, John F., *The Russian Conquest of the Caucasus* (London, 1908)

Baddeley, John F., *Russia, Mongolia, China*, 2 vols (London, 1919)

Caroe, Olaf, *Soviet Empire: The Turks of Central Asia and Stalinism* (London, 1953)

Chamberlin, William Henry, *The Russian Revolution 1917–1921*, 2 vols (New York, 1935)

Clark, Alan, *Barbarossa: The Russo-German Conflict 1941–1945* (London, 1965)

Conquest, Robert, *The Soviet Deportation of Nationalities* (London, 1960)

Cresson, W. P., *The Cossacks, their History and Country* (New York, 1919)

Dallin, Alexander, *German Rule in Russia 1941–1945*(London, 1957)

Dallin, David J., *The Rise of Russia in Asia* (London, 1950)

Dallin, David J. and Nicolaevsky, Boris I., *Forced Labour in Soviet Russia* (London, 1948)

Dixon, C. Aubrey and Heilbrunn, Otto, *Communist Guerilla Warfare* (London, 1954)

Dubnow, S. M., *History of the Jews in Russia and Poland* (Philadelphia, 1916–20)

Eudin, X. J. and Fisher, H. H., *Soviet Russia and the West 1920–1927: A Documentary Survey* (Stanford, 1957)

Fennell, J. L. I., *Ivan the Great of Moscow* (London, 1963)

Fennell, J. L. I., *The Emergence of Moscow 1304–1359* (London, 1968)

Fischer, Louis, *The Soviets in World Affairs*, 2 vols (London, 1930)

Fischer, Louis, *The Life of Lenin* (London, 1964)

Freund, Gerald, *Unholy Alliance: Russian-German Relations from the Treaty of Brest-Litovsk to the Treaty of Berlin* (London, 1957)

Futrell, Michael, *Northern Underground: Episodes of Russian Revolutionary Transport and Communications through Scandinavia and Finland 1863–1917* (London, 1963)

Greenberg, Louis, *The Jews in Russia: The Struggle For Emancipation*, 2 vols (New Haven, 1944, 1951)

Höhne, Heinz, *The Order of the Death's Head: The Story of Hitler's S.S.* (London, 1969)

Indian Officer, An (anon), *Russia's March Towards India*, 2 vols (London, 1894)

Jackson, W. A. Douglas, *Russo-Chinese Borderlands* (Princeton, 1962)

Joll, James, *The Anarchists* (London, 1964)

Kamenetsky, Ihor, *Hitler's Occupation of Ukraine 1941–1944: A Study of Totalitarian Imperialism* (Milwaukee, 1956)

Kazemzadeh, F., *The Struggle for Transcaucasia* (New York, 1951)

Katkov, George, *Russia 1917: The February Revolution* (London, 1967)

Kennan, George, *Siberia and the Exile System* (New York, 1891)

Kerner, Robert J., *The Urge to the Sea: The Course of Russian History* (Berkeley and Los Angeles, 1946)

Kirchner, Walther, *Commercial Relations Between Russia and Europe 1400 to 1800* (Bloomington, Indiana, 1966)

Klyuchevskii, Vasilii Osipovich, *Peter the Great* (London, 1958)

Kochan, Lionel, *Russia in Revolution 1890–1918* (London, 1966)

Kolarz, Walter, *Russia and her Colonies* (London, 1952)

Krypton, Constantine, *The Northern Sea Route* (New York, 1953)

Lang, D. M., *A Modern History of Georgia* (London, 1962)

Leslie, R. F., *Reform and Insurrection in Russian Poland* (London, 1963)

Lias, Godfrey, *Kazak Exodus* (London, 1956)

Liubavskii, M. K., *Ocherk Istorii Litovsko-Russkovo Gosudarstva* (Moscow, 1910; Russian Reprint Series, The Hague, 1966)

Lorimer, F., *The Population of the Soviet Union: History and Prospects* (Geneva, 1946)

Lyashchenko, Peter I., *History of the National Economy of Russia to the 1917 Revolution* (New York, 1949)

Maksimov, S., *Sibir i Katorga*, 3 vols (St Petersburg, 1871)

Malozemoff, A., *Russian Far Eastern Policy 1881–1904* (Los Angeles, 1958)

Manning, Clarence A., *Twentieth-Century Ukraine* (New York, 1951)

Mazour, Anatole G., *The First Russian Revolution, 1825: The Decembrist Movement* (Stanford, 1961)

Mikhailov, V., *Pamiatnaya Knizhka Sotsialista-Revoliutsionera*, 2 vols (Paris, 1911, 1914)

Miller, Margaret, *The Economic Development of Russia 1905–1914* (London, 1926)

Mora, Sylvestre and Zwierniak, Pierre, *La Justice Sovietique* (Rome, 1945)

Nasonov, A. N., *Russkaya Zemlia* (Moscow, 1951)

Nikitin, M. N. and Vagin, P. I., *The Crimes of the German Fascists in the Leningrad Region: Materials and Documents* (London, 1947)

Nosenko, A. K. (ed), *V. I. Lenin 1870–1924* (Kiev, n.d.). A collection of photographs, with 2 maps

Obolenski, Prince Eugene, *Souvenirs d'une Exilé en Sibérie* (Leipzig, 1862)

Owen, Launcelot A., *The Russian Peasant Movement 1906–17* (London, 1937)

Park, Alexander G., *Bolshevism in Turkestan 1917–1927* (New York, 1957)

Philippi, Alfred and Heim, Ferdinand, *Der Feldzug gegen Sowjetrussland 1941–1945* (Stuttgart, 1962)

Pierce, Richard A., *Russian Central Asia 1867–1917* (Berkeley and Los Angeles, 1960)

Pipes, Richard, *The Formation of the Soviet Union: Communism and Nationalism 1917–1923* (Cambridge, Massachusetts, 1954)

Platonov, S. F., *Ocherki Po Istorii Smuti v Moskovskom Gosudarstve* (Moscow, 1937)

Pospelov, P. N., *Istoriya Kommunisticheskoi Partii Sovetskovo Soyuza*, 6 vols (Moscow, 1964–8)

Pounds, Norman J. G., *Poland Between East and West* (Princeton, 1964)

Radkey, Oliver H., *The Agrarian Foes of Bolshevism* (New York, 1958)

Rapport du Parti Socialiste Revolutionnaire de Russie au Congres Socialiste International de Stuttgart (Ghent, 1907)

Reddaway, W. R., Penson, J. H., Halecki, O. and Dyboski, R. (eds), *Cambridge History of Poland*, 2 vols (Cambridge, 1941, 1950)

Reitlinger, Gerald, *The House Built on Sand: The Conflicts of German Policy in Russia 1939–1945* (London, 1960)

Riasanovsky, Nicholas V., *A History of Russia* (New York, 1963)

Rosen, Baron A., *Russian Conspirators in Siberia* (London, 1872)

Rostovtzeff, M., *The Iranians and Greeks in South Russia* (Oxford, 1922)

Salisbury, Harrison E., *The Siege of Leningrad* (London, 1969)

Schuyler, Eugene, *Peter the Great: Emperor of Russia*, 2 vols (London, 1844)

Schwarz, Solomon M., *The Russian Revolution of 1905* (Chicago, 1967)

Serge, Victor, *Memoirs of a Revolutionary 1901–1941* (London, 1963)

Seton-Watson, Hugh, *The Russian Empire 1801–1917* (London, 1967)

Shukman, Harold, *Lenin and the Russian Revolution* (London, 1966)

Simpson, Sir John Hope, *The Refugee Problem* (London, 1939)

Skazkin, S. D. (and others), *Istoriya Vizantii*, 3 vols (Moscow, 1967)

Slusser, Robert M. and Triska Jan F., *A Calendar of Soviet Treaties 1917–1957* (Stanford, 1959)

Squire, P. S., *The Third Department: The Establishment and Practices of the Political Police in the Russia of Nicholas I* (Cambridge, 1968)

Stephan, John J., *Sakhalin* (Oxford, 1971)

Sullivant, Robert S., *Soviet Politics and the Ukraine 1917–1957* (New York, 1962)

Sumner, B. H., *Peter the Great and the Ottoman Empire* (Oxford, 1949)

Sumner, B. H., *Peter the Great and the Emergence of Russia* (London, 1950)

Suprunenko, M. I. (and others), *Istoria Ukrainskoi RSR* (Kiev, 1958)

Tikhonov, Nikolai (and others), *The Defence of Leningrad: Eye-witness Accounts of the Siege* (London, 1944)

Treadgold, Donald W., *The Great Siberian Migration* (Princeton, 1957)

Trotsky, Leon, *My Life* (London, 1930)

Vernadsky, George, *The Mongols and Russia* (London, 1953)

Wheeler, G., *The Modern History of Soviet Central Asia* (London, 1964)

Woodward, David, *The Russians at Sea* (London, 1965)

Yarmolinski, Avram, *The Road to Revolution: A Century of Russian Radicalism* (London, 1957)

Yaroslavsky, E., *History of Anarchism in Russia* (London, 1937)

Zimin, A. A., *Reformy Ivana Groznovo* (Moscow, 1960)

(v) Articles

Anon., 'How the Bear Learned to Swim', *The Economist* (London, 24–30 October 1970)

Bealby, John Thomas, Kropotkin, Prince Peter Alexeivitch, Philips, Walter Alison and Wallace, Sir Donald Mackenzie, 'Russia', *The Encyclopaedia Britannica* (eleventh edition, London and New York, 1910)

Carsten, F. L., 'The Reichswehr and the Red Army 1920–1933', *Survey* (London, 1962)

Dziewanowski, M. K., 'Pilsudski's Federal Policy 1919–21', *Journal of Central European Affairs* (London, 1950)

Footman, David, 'Nestor Makno', *St Antony's Papers No. 6: Soviet Affairs No. 2* (Oxford, 1959)

Lobanov-Rostovsky, A., 'Anglo-Russian Relations through the Centuries', *Russian Review*, vol. 7 (New York, 1948)

Parkes, Harry, 'Report on the Russian Caravan Trade with China', *Journal of the Royal Geographic Society*, vol. 25 (London, 1854)

Stanhope, Henry, 'Soviet Strength at Sea', *The Times* (London, 25 January 1971)

Sullivan, Joseph L., 'Decembrists in Exile', *Harvard Slavic Studies*, vol. 4 (The Hague, 1954)

Wildes, Harry Emerson, 'Russia's Attempts to Open Japan', *Russian Review*, vol. 5 (New York, 1945)

Yakunskiy, V. K., 'La Révolution Industrielle en Russie', *Cahiers du Monde Russe et Sovietique* (The Hague, 1961)

Index